Having the courage, determination, and inner strength to endure. To undergo hardship without conceding, and to emerge as the Victor, instead of the victim

HELEN BRATHWAITE

I Will Survive
Having the courage, determination, and inner strength to endure. To undergo hardship without conceding, and to emerge as the Victor, instead of the victim

Copyright © 2022 by Helen Brathwaite.

Paperback ISBN: 978-1-63812-301-9
Ebook ISBN: 978-1-63812-300-2

All rights reserved. No part in this book may be produced and transmitted in any form or by any means, electronic, or mechanical, including photocopying, recording, or by any information storage and retrieval system, without permission in writing from the copyright owner.

The views expressed in this work are solely those of the author and do not necessarily reflect the views of the publisher hereby disclaims any responsibility for them.

Published by Pen Culture Solutions   07/27/2022

Pen Culture Solutions
1-888-727-7204 (USA)
1-800-950-458 (Australia)
support@penculturesolutions.com

To all my readers, It's been an honour and privilege that you have chosen to purchase this book. I hope that you will be inspired by reading its contents, as I have been to write it.

Thank you,
Helen Brathwaite.

Thank you to all those who've helped me with the entire production of this book. Leslie Cryer of The Writer's Bureau. Hayhouse: Reid Tracy and Kelly Notarus. Louise Hay and her book, "the power is within you." Nancy Levin, giving myself permission, and Kinko Hamilton, for giving me the encouragement to get my book published. To my entire family and all my friends, and to Mrs Valere, my English teacher at St Francois Girls College for the beginnings of my love of English and reading.

Chapter One

Trinidad and Tobago, land of the hummingbird, calypso, soca music, steel pans, and carnival, the most spectacular show on earth! Port Of Spain, Trinidad was where I was born on Monday the 20$^{th\,of}$ June 1955, and where I enjoyed the most idyllic of childhoods. Days spent going to school, playing cricket, boys against girls amongst the children in our neighbourhood.

Playing out in the rain, pretending to be cowboys and Indians hiding, surrounded by the banana trees in our garden. Imagining that we were shooting each other with imaginary guns. Climbing hills, spread out as it were, at the back of our street in Belmont. A suburb of Port of Spain. Returning home after hours spent outdoors with my brothers, sisters, and friends, with growling stomachs, bruised, grazed knees, soiled, and / or torn clothing.

An independent, English-speaking nation, within the commonwealth. Comprised of people of African, Indian, Chinese, European, Middle Eastern, and mixed races. Resulting in multi-cultural, religious groups. Roman Catholics, Anglicans, Hindus, Muslims, and others. With the most delicious, tasty, colourful, and mouth-watering foods. The nation`s favourite dishes being roti. A flour and split pea type flat bread. Cooked on the cooker top, over a medium heat setting. Served with curried meat and potatoes. Doubles, two inner surfaces of the hand size flour/ split pea flatbreads, with curried chickpeas between them. Chicken pelau, a mixture of chicken, rice, and pigeon or gunga peas. Immensely popular too, is scooping out the jelly of the coconut, after drinking it`s water. Purchased from vendors around the Queen`s Park Savannah. The largest park, and the biggest traffic roundabout in the world.

The twin island, the most southern in the Caribbean. Just seven miles off the Venezuelan coast. Enjoy a warm, sunny, climate throughout the year. The average temperature, being twenty-eight degrees centigrade. There are two seasons, the dry, from January through to May. The rainy, from June to December. It has always thrilled me, even as a child, driving with my parents, and siblings, to Maracas Beach. On the North coast of the island. An hour's drive from the city of Port of Spain. Along the narrow, hilly, winding, picturesque road, where on one side, there's a sharp drop to the sea below. There's a popular viewing vantage point on the way there, where magnificent, panoramic views exist. The opacity of the clear, blue sky, and the serenity, and stillness of the aquamarine waters, very gently flowing below it.

At the beach, the waves lap against the golden sand. Leaving behind the greenish, bluish, waters of the sea. The crescent shaped bay, with its coconut trees, moving in the breezy, sunshine, with lush rainforest cliffs in the background. After an enjoyable swim, there are vendors, selling bake and shark. Freshly made melt in your mouth rolls and fried shark. Served with salad, and varying sauces. Washed down with soft drinks, from several food huts stretched along the sand.

Visiting the Asa Wright nature resort, and scientific research centre in Arima. Walking amongst the enchanting terrain of The Northern Range, was a pleasure to do. Following our family's group introductory talk at the main house. We set off in smaller groups, led by tour guides. It is one of the best bird watching experiences in The Caribbean, with 256 species present. There are also various agricultural exhibits on display, being the most biodiverse in the region. All this vast expanse of land comes with an inn and restaurant. Making it even more appealing for its guests, as it serves produce from the centre's own organic gardens. Our visit ended with us savouring a very welcome and tasty afternoon tea.

Considered by villagers to be the eighth wonder of the world. The pitch lake in the village of La Brea carries that honour. At first sight it looks rather unattractive, but that is very much far from the truth. Our tour began at the lake's entrance, from whence our guide escorted us on a tour across the sea of asphalt, following an introductory talk. It produces dark, clay like substances, some of them increasing or decreasing in size. We were very grateful to be in the guide's care, as some parts were unsafe to walk on. As we walked, we heard hissing sounds, most likely due to the levels of natural activity in the soil. My daughter Natalie couldn't help herself, splashing in one of the pools of water. Accumulated during the rainy season. It was reported to have high levels of sulphur, wonderful for treating ailments like joint pain. We left with small samples of asphalt, of which some is used locally, and some exported for the paving of roads worldwide.

Tobago's Crown Point International Airport, only a twenty-minute flight from Piarco International Airport in Port of Spain. A stone's throw away is Store Bay. A small white sandy beach, with deck chairs and umbrellas spread out along the sand. For the benefit and enjoyment of its guests. The bay's clear blue sea welcomes regular daily glass bottomed boats, pulled unto the shore, as much as possible, so that visitors can climb into the vessels. Wading knee deep, to waist high through the body of water. Which allows everyone seated inside them, to see the beauty of Buccoo Reef.

Another pick up area is Pigeon Point. Store Bay's next door neighbour. Another beautiful beach with matching white sands, and blue sea. From here, visitors to the reef can board the boats, from an attractive, quaint, thatched roof jetty.

Buccoo Reef is a protected coral, and marine underwater patch, with a captivating array of colours of sea life. Leaving the safety of the boats behind, we were able to swim and snorkel around, observing its natural beauty. The water is shallow to accommodate this pleasure. Laying behind this splendour, is Nylon Pool. Another shallow stretch of water, also containing coral. Everyone is encouraged to have a relaxing swim in the warm, clear blue, still, lagoon. Where we were able to comfortably stand, even though we were far away from the shore.

Centuries ago, when the European countries of Holland, France, Spain, and England, fought over the various islands in the West Indies. The English built forts. Fortified look out points, to avoid capture. With one in Port of Spain, and the other in Scarborough, Tobago.

Being a multicultural nation. The festivities of each group are celebrated. The Hindu festival of light Diwali, Eid, for Muslims. For Christians, Easter and Christmas. As the Christmas festivities end, the preparations for carnival begin. The calypso tents are again running, just as all musical events begin, with masquerade bands planning ideas for their costumes. The Steel bands also begin practising in earnest, in readiness for Panorama.

The steel orchestra competition. The final, of which is held on the Saturday night the celebrations begin on the carnival Monday and Tuesday, before Ash Wednesday each year.

On this very Saturday afternoon, is the kiddie's carnival. On the Sunday, the king and queen of the bands takes place. With each contestant portraying their own colourful, painstakingly well-made costumes, conveying a particular subject matter, before a packed televised audience, and judges. The crowning of the soca monarch follows, in an evening of entertaining performances of calypso/soca music.

J'ouvert begins just before dawn. Revellers dressed in old clothing, covered in grease, paint, and chocolate, dancing through the streets until the sun appears. As the day breaks, thousands of other merry makers flood the streets. There's a release of colour! A dancing, happy throng. Throbbing and pulsating with energy, and activity. Accompanied by soca music from speakers on music trucks. The music tempting and awakening further joy in everyone.

On the following morning, carnival Tuesday. The celebrations continue. The bands parading along the routes and judging points of the city. The ranges of colour! The imagination! The thought processes! The ability to make and create original pieces of art and craft, evidenced by these costumes, simply takes your breath away.

I'd always had that stubborn, determined, streak as far back as I can remember. My fourth birthday was approaching, and I was very keen on having a party. Disappointed when my request was denied by my parents. I waited until the day before my birthday, to invite my entire nursery school class, including the teacher to my party, which went ahead as I'd anticipated.

Our family moved to 5 Lenore Street Belmont, when I was five years old. My brothers were enrolled at Eastern boys' government school, and my sisters and I began to attend Eastern girls' government school. We learnt spelling and times tables by rote. Even singing little songs, so that we could remember them. Woe betides anyone who got it wrong. That person would be smacked on their knuckles with a ruler. Or made to sit all alone in the classroom at breaktime. Being called "duncy head" by their class-mates. No one wanted that to happen to them.

It was Friday the 31st August 1962. The day of our nation's independence from the United Kingdom. It was a day of rampant celebrations throughout the land. Regardless of the school holidays, we were all there partying. Singing and dancing along to the music. Playing games, and eating ice cream and cake. All in all, having a wonderful time.

Our sister Lois, born on the 17$^{th\,of}$ September 1962 became the new addition to the family of Pam, Pat, Judy, Helen, Charles, and Skippy. There was no shortage of offers to feed, change, bath, and take her for walks in her pram. September the 26th 1963 dawned very windy, and rainy. There was much anticipation that Hurricane Flora was on her way. We were taken home from school just after lunch by our father as there were raging winds and torrential rain. All schools and businesses were closed, and everyone was advised to stay at home. As youngsters we didn't fully understand the seriousness of the situation. As the gales and water battered against the windowpanes, and our mother settled us down to bed that evening. We pleaded with her. "Please wake us when the hurricane comes."

My parents were involved in the church. My mother Dearest was the organist, and my father Cecil the choir master. Therefore, we as children spent most of our young lives in church. Attending Sunday school, girls club, boys club, girls brigade, and young people's groups. My father also sang in various choirs, and groups in Port of Spain.

At Christmas each year, all the children in our neighbourhood would be busy saving up their pocket money, to buy and collect hand held sparklers. To be lit up on the evening of Christmas Eve. What a joy it was to run up and down our street, holding our lit star shaped sparks of light. Shrieking with delight, as we threw our almost extinguished products into the expectant twilight air. Finally going to bed in our newly decorated home, as everyone in the country painted their dwellings, in the run up to the festive season. Eager and watchful than we were the day before. Hoping to catch a glimpse of Santa Claus. Following breakfast, we would visit my mother's sister and her husband, Aunty Prince and Uncle CB. Then spend the rest of the day with our grandparents Carmen, Garnet, and my father's sister, Aunty Oddie, and her husband Uncle Leroy.

My mother and her sister became orphans at a young age. Therefore, they were brought up by her mother's brother, Uncle Alan, and his wife, Aunty Thelma. Uncle Alan was a musician, and was gifted in being able to play most, if not all musical instruments. He had in his possession, one of those old pianos, which held two candlesticks, and an antique double bass, which had been imported from Germany. My mother and her sister were also musicians. During school holidays, our time would be divided between visiting all our close family.

My grandmother would cook us each whatever we wanted to eat. We were both fond of baking, and I would help her with the task. I even had my own set of mini baking tins. It was February 1966. The Queen and Prince Philip were on a state visit to our country, as part of a Caribbean tour. Port of Spain's Queen's Park Oval was jam packed, with very keen, eager school children. Intent on impressing the royal couple, with their well-rehearsed display of singing and dancing. Enthusiastically waving our flags, cheering them on to the covered podium, from where they would sit to enjoy the pageant.

At this point, the blue skies and the sun had completely disappeared. Replaced by dark clouds, and rain. Most of the primary school children were positioned in the uncovered stands of the venue. We were all drenched. Then just as dramatically, the clear blue skies, and an abundance of sunshine dried our bodies. Resulting in our entire class displaying symptoms of a cold. At least we were able to proudly boast, that we sang for The Queen, and Prince Philip.

As an eleven year old pupil of Standard Five. I was preparing once again for the eleven plus examination, which on passing well ensured passage into one of the best high schools in the country. This was my second attempt. I was full of a cold at my first attempt. Not doing myself much justice. Our class teacher, Mrs Lucille Archibald, coached us in the morning before school, and after our lessons had ended for the day. All that hard work was recompensed by a 100% pass rate. We were all thrilled with our results. I'd been accepted at the high school of my first choice, St Francois Girls College of Belmont, Port of Spain.

My five years at the college began in September 1967. The school was opened in 1962, in the year of our independence from the UK. It was the only government grammar school for girls in the country. The principal being Mrs Gloria T Valere. The daughter of the late Sir Learie Constantine. International West Indian cricketer, lawyer, and politician, who served as The High Commissioner for Trinidad and Tobago, and the UK's first black peer.

Situated on St Francois Valley Road, Belmont, with each side of the slightly hilly driveway, leading up to the school. Benefiting from well maintained lawns, flowers, and trees. The various classrooms elegantly, and spaciously spread out amongst the undulating fields. My teachers appeared to have great difficulty in remembering my name. My two eldest sisters, Pam and Pat, were also pupils there. Eventually, they settled to calling me Miss Mottley.

My first Friday morning's class was religious education. Mrs Maynard was our teacher. A lovely, kind, middle-aged, well-dressed lady, who loved to sing. She always started her lesson by singing "The king of love my shepherd is," in a rather croaky voice. It wasn't my intention to laugh, but when snickering began to be stifled in areas across the room, I just couldn't help it. I began to laugh, and laugh, till I couldn't stop! I continued to laugh even after I'd arrived at Mrs Valere's office, with tears rolling down my cheeks, after being sent there by Mrs Maynard.

Being active with the Girls Brigade, as a brigader in the 11th Trinidad Company, and being a member of my school's choir kept me very busy. Our choir was diligently practising for our entry to the Trinidad and Tobago music festival. After lots of hard work, we emerged winners of The Judge Russel Cup.

Mrs Valere had called our school year to heel once again. Observing that we were chatting, laughing, and telling joke after joke, when we were supposed to be studying for our upcoming G.C.E "O" Level examinations, set and marked by Cambridge University England. Reminding us of the value of adequate preparations, and the remarkable effects that that could have on our results. I've never forgotten these words. "If you fail to prepare, prepare to fail."

I wasn't keen on pursuing "A" Level studies, but more interested in nursing. Deciding to apply to hospitals in England. All aspects of education were controlled from the UK. Our exams were set and marked by Cambridge University. Our music from The Royal School of Music and Trinity College of Music in London. I wanted to see where all these places were.

Following months of applying to several hospitals. Then being required to write an essay on "my family." In order to provide evidence that I was fully in command of the English language, which I'd spoken all my life. Finally, I was accepted to commence student nurse training on Monday the 5th ^{of} May 1975. At Amersham and High Wycombe School of Nursing.

During this time, I worked temporarily as a clerical assistant, for a publishing company. Longman's Caribbean. Also employed at St Georges Primary School, after school club. I also became a member of a singing group of teenagers, hosting several concerts in Port of Spain.

Following months of planning, including having medicals, blood tests, X rays, police security checks, vaccinations, obtaining a student's entry visa for the United Kingdom. On the evening of the 27th ^{of} April 1975, I left Trinidad for London, England, as a passenger on BWIA flight nine hundred. I managed to hold my nerve bidding my family farewell. It took a magnitude of inner strength and aptitude, to leave them behind at the departure gate, without shedding a tear. As soon as I was strapped in my seat, with no one around me to notice. The tears really began to flow. Once again, silently and in loneliness.

The aircraft taxied along the runway, in preparation for take-off, when it abruptly stopped for no apparent reason. My father began to panic. Enquiring of the BWIA personnel what exactly had happened. The captain had forgotten his belongings. Then finally with very mixed emotions of anticipation, and excitement, integrated with sadness. The great adventure of my life began.

Chapter Two

Finally, the over-night flight from Port of Spain, had landed at Heathrow Airport. The doors to the aircraft were opened, with a portable steel staircase placed in position. Enabling the boarding of the passengers from the airliner to some buses, lying in wait for transportation to the nearby terminal buildings.

Bleary eyed but bushy tailed, I emerged from the aeroplane, having hardly slept, with eyes red and bulging, from crying throughout the night. Intriguingly, I noticed misty smoke like vapours escaping through my lips, as I made my way down the steps. Finding it even more interesting, that the hazy suspension flowing through the air, was my own breath.

I couldn't help but shiver, in the early morning spring sunshine, before boarding the bus. However, there was a vast difference between the weather in Trinidad and Tobago, and England. My great adventure had indeed begun. Being sad at leaving home, but so excited at the prospect of what lay ahead.

I fleetingly stopped in anxious hesitation and anticipation, as I strode into the arrival's hall. Someone from the hospital was supposed to be meeting me there. I noticed that there were two rows of people, one on each side of two metal barriers, leading into the arrival's hall itself. I walked along that route, hoping that my name, would be on one of two written notices, that I'd seen at the end of the rows.

On the left-hand side, stood a middle-aged man, as thin as a string of spaghetti, with his dark brown receding hairline, almost touching the ceiling. His large hands bore a poster with the name Helen Mottley written on it.

After greeting each other. We were required to wait for two male students from Mauritius, who were starting their nurse training at the same time, and at the same hospital as I was, and whose flight had arrived forty-five minutes after mine. We were about to begin our training on Monday the 5th of May 1975, at Amersham and High Wycombe school of nursing, based at Wycombe General Hospital, High Wycombe, Buckinghamshire. Twenty-nine miles from London, and Amersham General Hospital, Amersham, Buckinghamshire. Twenty-seven miles from London, and thirteen from High Wycombe.

Eagerly awaiting my arrival at Wycombe General Hospital's Groveland's Nurses Home was Umilta Daniels. Senior ward sister of 5A, female surgical ward. Originally from Port of Spain, Trinidad. She was my mother's friend. Someone I'd known since I was a little girl. She took me under her wing, helping me to find my bearings around the large, industrial, and hilly market town.

Getting there seven days prior to commencement of training, to familiarise myself with my new surroundings. I continually felt cold, and lonely in my room. I was missing my large family tremendously. My home life, where it was always so noisy, with so many people about. All alone in my room. It was so eerily quiet! Everything just felt so strange. Even though I was always overdressed with jumpers, not normally worn at that time of year. I found it necessary to switch on the overhead heater, lying in situ just above my bed. The radiators were switched off, as the month of May had just begun.

Very quickly I became friends with Joanna. My next-door neighbour, a staff nurse of six months. "I don't know what I'm going to do with my record player. I'm moving to Birmingham in a few days, and I'm not taking it as I'm getting a new one." As quick as a flash, I said, "Can I have it? How much do you want for it?" "You can have it" she said. "Have you been to Birmingham Helen?" asked Janet. One of Joanna's friends, Janet was moving to London in a few days to also commence her midwifery training. "No, I've never been to Birmingham." I replied. "Would you like to come with us to help Joanna move her things?" "Thank you. I'd love to." I answered.

As an enthusiastic music fan, I was delighted with my merchandise. I knew that that would be the perfect solution, for my blossoming desire to return home. I could always rely on my music to cheer me up.

Within the next few days, four girls from Zimbabwe, Carol, Priscah, Terri, and Elisheba, Laye Khim from Brunei, and Eliza from Sri Lanka, had arrived in the nurses' home. We were all due to start our training together. I would continually take my player into the kitchen, as I was cooking to sing and dance to the music, to improve my feeling of despair. I reminded myself, that I came to England to study nursing, and that was what I was going to do. No matter what! I constantly reassured myself, "I'll be all right. I'll soon get used to it." I was determined to stick it out. Family and friends were anxious for my welfare, and didn't believe that I'd make it. I intended to prove them wrong.

Quite often, the other girls couldn't resist joining in with my singing, dancing, laughing, and joking around in the kitchen. We would end up having little dinner parties in each other's rooms, sampling, and savouring our individual, national, culinary dishes. Exploring the music, and cultures of our countries. I was always the one who cheered everyone up, with jokes, and unwavering laughter and positivity.

I was one of a group of eighteen student nurses. Nine English, and nine over-seas. One from Sri Lanka, one from Brunei, four from Zimbabwe, two from Mauritius, and yours truly from Trinidad. Monday the 5th of May 1975 was spent being introduced to each other, and our tutors. Registering for national insurance contributions, surgeries, dentists. Getting to meet several female students from previous groups, who instructed us, how to fold our nurses' caps, into a butterfly shape at the back of it.

There was an initial eight-week training programme, called the introductory block. The English students would sit on one side of the room, whilst the rest of us would sit on the other. We learnt about various aspects of nursing. Including bed bathing, bed making, giving injections, checking, and recording temperatures, pulse, respiration, and anatomy and physiology.

Our eight-week course was ending. I was one of the nine students, commencing their training at Amersham General Hospital, for a period of eighteen months. Followed by a further eighteen months at Wycombe General Hospital.

There was a loud knock at the door of my room. It was Maureen Porter, the home warden. "There's a Jeanette Sowerbutts on the phone for you." She stated. Hurriedly I ran along in quick succession to Mrs Porter's office to receive my call.

"Hi Helen. It's Jeanette Sowerbutts. I've made arrangements for a Mrs Diane Smith, captain of The Girls Brigade in Amersham, to meet, and bring you to the Royal Albert Hall, for our Girls Brigade concert." Being an active member of the Girls Brigade in Trinidad. A member of the 11th Trinidad Company. Having met Jeanette on previous official visits to the island. As soon as she'd heard that I was coming to England. She'd invited me to this special event, where all U.K companies were converging.

Amersham, a market town in the Chiltern district of the county of Buckinghamshire. Lying to the Northwest of London. The last stop on the Metropolitan Line of the London Underground. Consists of two areas. Old Amersham, where Amersham General Hospital was situated, and Amersham on the Hill, where the underground, and main line station existed.

For students to become acquainted to life on the wards, two visits were arranged to each of their first allocations. First, an early shift, from the hours of 07.45 till 1630 hours. Then a late work period, from 12.30 P.M till 2045hours, during the last few weeks of the introductory block.

Dressed in my Girls Brigade Trinidad uniform. I was met at the High Street, Old Amersham, by The Girls Brigade captain, Diane Smith, and all the members of her company. Clothed in their U.K attire. Theirs being of thicker material, including blazers, to suit the colder weather conditions. We greeted each other warmly, before taking our seats. As the coach set off for the capital city. A pleasant, rapid exchange of questions, and answers began. Interestingly about the differences of life experiences in our countries. All the while, observing the landmarks, as we got into London, approaching South Kensington.

The Royal Albert Hall appeared just as it did, after having seen televised shows from the venue. It was the same famous, esteemed building. Opened by Queen Victoria in 1871. With its Greek amphitheatre designed build. There were coaches everywhere. Dropping off girls from every part of the country. There waiting for me, was Jeanette Sowerbutts, who informed me that I was to be her guest of honour.

A slight brief feeling of self-consciousness enveloped me, as I was requested to stand to be greeted, and applauded by everyone. After being introduced to them, the lights were dimmed, welcoming in the wonderful evening's entertainment.

Walking from Chenies Nurses Home, across the car park, making my way down the hilly, slanting corridor. Up the side of a hill, with wards, and departments, their spider like arms linked by its body, the main pathway. I walked down to the bottom of the passageway to female surgical, A Ward. With my first-year student nurses' uniform in pristine condition. My brown leather shoes polished, and shining to perfection. Portraying my own reflection in them. My nurses' cap superbly folded into a butterfly shape. I was dreading my first day at work, following my introductory block. Hoping that Sr. Wright wouldn't be on duty.

I'd met her on my first visit. Where she stood erect. Only five feet, five inches tall. Shoulders held back. Chest pushed forwards. Looking and sounding like an army sergeant major. I was in total awe of her then. And in dread of her now. Being so relieved to work with Staff Nurse Robinson, who was to chaperone me throughout our early shift.

There were beds to be made. Bed baths to be given. Wounds to be dressed Temperatures, pulses, and blood pressures to be checked, and recorded. Patients to be prepared for theatre. Ensuring, and recording that they'd had nothing to eat or drink six hours before surgery. That their identity bracelets carried the correct information about them. That all clothing, hair clips, nail varnish, jewellery, dentures, were removed. That they were dressed in theatre gown, and cap. That the consent form was signed by the patient. That the premedication, the drugs administered to sedate, and prepare them for general anaesthetic was given and recorded.

On returning from the operation, there was regular checking, and recording of temperature, pulse, blood pressure. Observing the wound for any excessive bleeding. Any abnormalities indicative of shock. Noting that the Intra Venous Infusion was running satisfactorily. That urinary output was within normal limits. Ensuring that pain relief was adequate, and that the patient was comfortable.

Even though Staff Nurse Robinson was the perfect mentor, I felt very unsure of myself. It was embarrassing not hearing Mrs Brown's blood pressure recording, whilst attempting to check it. "Don't worry about it.

You'll soon pick it up." She reassured me. The other student from my group, Barbara Young, appeared to be so self-assured. Darting here, there, and everywhere. Brimming with confidence.

Waiting for the lift, on the ground floor at Chenies, was Lillian Johnstone. A middle-aged woman, from Trinidad. Working as an enrolled nurse on night duty. She was always smartly and elegantly dressed. With friendly, twinkling eyes. Short-cropped hair, and the warmest of smiles. She held a tray in her hands, on which there were two dishes, covered with foil.

As I approached her, she greeted me with these words. "Hello Helen. There's some people I'd love you to meet." There was an incessant sound of laughter, happy voices, and the waft of delicious, home–cooked food, coming from the direction of her room. Even as we approached it from the lift.

As we opened the door to her room. There was already a spread of mouth-watering cuisine on her coffee table. The steam of which was rising like a genie ascending from a bottle, in the middle of Lillian's room. Over a meal of macaroni pie, rice and peas, chicken, vegetables, and salad. I came to know Lilla Patrick, thirty years old. A midwife at Amersham, from Grenada, who had the wonderful knack of having everyone doubled up with laughter, as she told jokes, without even the trace of a smile on her face. Sybil Harris, about thirty-five years old, from Barbados, also a midwife at Amersham. Sybil had the most infectious of laughs, which set me off, with tears rolling down my cheeks.

"Nurse Mottley!" Boomed the roaring sound of Sister Wright's voice. Thundering down the corridor of the Nightingale ward. Named after Florence Nightingale. Consisting of one large main ward, with a few side rooms for patients. Sluice, the ward kitchen, staff toilets, and ward office. I stood to attention in the middle of the main ward. My feet appearing to be stuck to the floor. Unable to utter a sound. The eyes of the patients, nurses, and doctors pointing in my direction. "Sorry Sister. It wasn't Nurse Mottley. I was the one who left the bowl in the sink." Admitted Student Nurse Winstanley.

Without a word, Sister Wright took to her heels. Disappearing into her office. Closely followed by Vera Thompson, a retired ward sister, who was a patient on the ward, and the consultant, Mr Lamb. I vanished into the sanctuary of the sluice. Closing the door firmly behind me. The sound of raised voices began to escape from the office. Busily tidying, and cleaning all the cupboards, commodes, bedpans. Putting away mouth wash bowls and cups, to recapture my composure. As I sang, jigging along to one of my favourite calypsos. The 1974 hit by Shadow. "Pom, pom, pom, pi, ti, pom, pom, pom, pi, ti, pom, pom, pom, pom, pom, pom, pom, pom, I was planning to forget calypso and go and plant peas in Tobago.,"

My third wage packet of £75 had arrived, following deductions for my NHS pension scheme, accommodation, taxes, and national insurance. An entire supermarket's shop cost £4.00. A cinema ticket was priced at ten pence. Sixty pence was all it required, to travel the entire length of The London Underground. This left a lot of money in reserve for a rainy day. "You're very lucky to be starting just as we've gotten a pay rise, courtesy of Barbara Castle," said Staff Nurse Ann Smith, as we examined our pay slips during our coffee break.

The latest off duty was up for inspection on the notice board, in the ward office. I breathed a sigh of relief, when I realised that I was to be working under Sister Matthews, the junior sister. "I guess the sluice won't be as sparkling as it is now." Declared Anna, with a chuckle. It was no secret, that I avoided as much contact as possible with Sister Wright. She appeared to shout at me at every opportunity. Her presence terrified me. Once there was a lull in ward activities, I'd seek solace in the sluice, cleaning everything till it shone. Simply to be out of her way. Sister Matthews had completed my ward report. Signing my student nurses progress booklet, indicating all the procedures that I'd witnessed, or participated in. I was due to move forward to my second ward. C Ward, female medical.

Almost falling over rushing to get the bus to High Wycombe. I turned the corner of the old hospital building, built in 1838/39. This was situated just beyond the hospital's entrance. There was the bus driving past, and almost at the stop, indirectly opposite the health facility. The driver must have seen me frantically flapping my arms, bird like through the air. Whilst sprinting the short distance across the road, to the bus stop. I couldn't thank him enough for waiting for me.

Boarding the vehicle, slightly out of breath. Ready to take my seat, to drive through the picturesque villages between Amersham and High Wycombe. My friend, Hermes Heath was arriving from New York this afternoon. All ready and waiting to commence her student nurse training, at the beginning of September 1975. I wanted to be there at the hospital to welcome her.

C Ward, of similar design to A Ward, was managed by two sisters. Senior Sister Whitely, about fifty years old. Her hair matching her name. Forever smiling, pleasant, and approachable, but commanded respect. The junior sister, Sister Neville about thirty years old. Very slender, wearing her sister's belt, with silver buckle, tightly wrapped around her tiny waist.

The work-load was heavy, demanding, but none the less rewarding. Nursing patients with medical conditions, including cerebral vascular accidents, (strokes) high blood pressure, and diabetes. It was an opportunity to learn more about each patient's individual health conditions. About their health needs, and how they could be met. Learning to have empathy with them. To be understanding, and compassionate. It was what nursing was all about. Encouraging, and helping them to feed themselves, as their condition improved. Maintaining and recording fluid intake, and output. Caring for those who weren't able to mobilise effectively. Helping them to change positions, to avoid the occurrence of pressure sores.

Sitting bolt upright in bed. I began to shiver. My room was so cold, and dark. For a moment, I couldn't remember exactly where I was. I couldn't see anything. Not even my alarm clock. "What time is it? Will I be late for work again?" I asked myself. As if on cue, it came to life. It was 6.30A.M. Time to get ready for work.

I hated the early morning shift. Especially at this time of year. It was now autumn, with the night's drawing in, and the mornings cold and dark. Fortunately, I lived in the nurses' home. Not having far to walk to get to the wards. My thick navy blue/red nurses' cape wrapped tightly around my shoulders, keeping me warm.

It was on C Ward that I met Grace Derby. A staff Nurse from Barbados. We'd worked together on numerous occasions. Advising, and guiding me, each time we worked together. Hermes had now completed her eight-week introductory block and was beginning her eighteen-month stint at Amersham. Joanna Tung, and Annie Ho, both second year students from Malaysia, who were working with me on C Ward, had invited us for a Chinese meal in Annie's room. "Pow!" (A Chinese steamed bun filled with meat or vegetables. Exceedingly popular in Trinidad and Tobago.)

Exclaimed Hermes and I in unison. We were thrilled to see it amongst the selection of dishes on display on her coffee table.

Spellbound, I carefully treaded my way across the car park. Falling behind the others, on our way to work. Closely watching the small, fluffy like flakes of snow, drifting feather-like from the skies above, to the earth below. This was my first experience of these phenomena. Having a few days earlier confusing ground frost with snow.

Hermes and I were almost attempting a hundred metre dash across the car park to Chenies. We were rushing off duty from our early shifts, the tantalising aroma of Caribbean cooking, tenderly being prepared in the oven. Drifting from the ground floor kitchen, tempting our taste buds. As we waited for the lift to appear. There was the jolly sound of Pat's voice, and Sybil's infectious laughter, coming from the direction of the second floor, where they both lived.

We were due to gather there for our Sunday lunch. Pat, Sybil, Hermes, Lilly, (a student midwife from Jamaica,) Lillian, and I. Relaxed after our meal, with jokes flowing continuously amongst us. I quipped in. "Would you like to hear a dirty joke?" "What do you know about dirty jokes? "Pat asked. "A white horse fell in a pool of mud." I stated. A moment of total silence eclipsed Pat's room before the acknowledgement of my supposedly humorous remark. Prompting the origination of my nickname. "White horse."

It was Sister Mehta who welcomed me to theatre. She was of Indian origin, medium height, and rather slim. She kindly and patiently taught me the scrubbing and gowning technique, about instruments, and theatre packs, and their sterilisation, and the importance of a clean, and sterile working environment.

I'd been invited to spend Christmas with Auntie Gwen, my mother's friend, who lived in Upminster, Essex. It was to be my first Christmas away from home. All I could think of was Trinidad and being with my family. Sitting on the underground train, on the way to Upminster. I was so grateful to Auntie Gwen, and her daughter Caroline, for helping to fill that void.

My first year was rapidly coming to an end. I was currently working on children's ward, my fourth and final allocation for that year. It was 1976. My parent's twenty fifth anniversary was being celebrated on the 24th of

March. I was longing to be present for the occasion, but wasn't on holiday at that time. Being almost halfway through a ward placement, and due to have three weeks vacation at the end of my first year. Discussing the dilemma with my tutors. My appointment on children's ward was equally split into two. My three weeks leave placed in the middle.

"Little Nurse Mottley can you collect these items from pharmacy and path. Lab? "Asked Sister Robertson, handing me a list of what she required. "But Sister Robertson, I'm about to start taking the temperatures, according to the ward workbook. I'm responsible for doing them this afternoon." I pleaded with her. "Don't worry about it. I'll ask Nurse Roberts to do them for you." She stated.

Aware that I was now back on the ward. Putting away the things which I'd collected from the two departments. Student Nurse Roberts remarked within my earshot, that she'd been asked to check temperatures. A job she thought was beneath her status, as a third-year student nurse, about to take her final exams. "I wish some people would do their jobs properly." She said with utter contempt in her voice. "Are you speaking to me?" I asked her. "If I hadn't been sent on errands here, there, and everywhere. Then I would have been able to carry out my work to everyone's satisfaction." All the medical, and nursing staff present in the ward office, gathered there for the afternoon's ward round, enquiringly wandered into the corridor. Perplexed as to what was happening in the treatment room. Incredibly surprised to find that my normally placid tone of voice was rising rapidly. To their astonishment, I grabbed hold of my handbag. Furiously draping my nurses' cape around my shoulders. Saying "I'll see you all tomorrow. "They all watched me with a look of utter bewilderment on their faces. Their mouths almost touching the floor. As I vanished swiftly through the ward's entrance. Strangely enough nothing was mentioned about the incident on the following day. Nor was I ever expected to repeat these tasks again.

A feeling of immense pleasure and joy came over me, as my BWIA flight began making it's descent into Port of Spain. Strapped into my window seat, I was continually straining, and stretching my neck, to see every vantage point possible, on the way there. The five islands lying in The Gulf of Paria. The Queen's Park Savannah. Till the aircraft touched down at the airport.

My two eldest sisters, Pam and Pat were there to meet me for my surprise visit to 'Trinidad and Tobago. They were the only ones who knew of my arrival. My mother repeatedly blinked and rubbed her eyes as she lay in bed resting recovering from a cold. She kept saying repeatedly. "It can't be Helen. She's in England. I must be dreaming." It wasn't until I began laughing that she knew that I was there in person in her bedroom. She was at once better. Rearranging a party that she'd postponed due to sickness. Now overflowing with happiness. I then visited our next-door neighbours. Mrs Rivers, and Mrs Awon, incapacitated in bed with the virus. Both immediately out of bed, and better as soon as they saw me.

There were shouts of elation, and tears as my father, siblings, and neighbours, returned home from work and school. My father brought his car to an immediate stand still. With the engine running as soon as he'd noticed me standing at the doorway of our kitchen. He, and my youngest sister, Lois rushed to greet me, with tears running down their cheeks.

The three weeks simply flew. With outings to Maracas Beach, enjoying bake and shark, chicken roti, and doubles, coconut water encapsulated within the coconut, purchased from vendors around the savannah. Also attending The Trinidad and Tobago music festival competition. My friend Hyacinth Nicholls had won a scholarship to study music in England, because of being one of the most outstanding winners of the competition.

It was wonderful meeting all my school friends once again. Attending our school's, St Francois Girls College sports day. Mrs Valere, our principal, enquired how I was faring with my studies, and life in England. Most of all it was a privilege, an honour, and a blessing, to be present at the party for family and friends, celebrating my parents silver wedding anniversary.

Developing a cold a few days before returning to Amersham, as feelings of homesickness gathered momentum. It took a great deal of will power, and inner strength, for me to return there, to finish my course. My ears began to ache mercilessly, as my BWIA flight began its descent into London Heathrow. With each twinge, my ears throbbed. With seat belt fastened, I leaned forward, then backwards. Sweating profusely. In co-ordination with the origin of the pain. With each body movement, my tears began to flow in silence down my cheeks.

"Is everything O.K?" the steward asked me. "My ears are sore, with a feeling of pressure, and pain inside them." I answered." "Chew on this. It will help to relieve the pressure, and pain inside your ears." She reassured me, as she offered me a stick of chewing gum. On this I chewed. As though my life depended on it. Until the aircraft came to a complete standstill on the tarmac of the airport. This hurting continued for a week, following my arrival back in Amersham. Enforcing a week's leave of absence from working on Children's ward.

Chapter Three

"Good morning, Sister Slater. I'm Student Nurse Mottley. I'll be working here for ten weeks, and this is my first day." I announced brightly, introducing myself to her.

She was about thirty. Dangling her legs from the edge of her position on her swivel chair, beside her desk. There was no reply. At first, I was unsure whether she'd heard me. Then I realised that she was listening. There was a stubborn look on her face. One that was unwilling to encourage any form of contact. It was as though I'd become invisible to her. She never acknowledged me.

There was a deafening silence in the room. Everyone present for the ward hand over appeared to be ill at ease. I became unsure of what to do or say. Standing forlornly in the middle of the ward office. Thankfully, Staff Nurse Bowen came to my rescue. Along with a generous smile on her face. "You'll be working with me today. Nurse Mottley" She informed me.

The West Indies cricket team were touring England that long, sweltering summer. Whilst I was working on male surgical, D Ward, the first of my second year. There was always banter amongst the patients and I. Always about cricket. That England would beat The West Indies.

Sister Slater continued to ignore me. Even as we'd worked together a few times. There was never an attempt made to have a conversation between us. There was no such problem between Sister Gillibrand and me.

Hermes and I had gone to London for the day. We were standing on the pavement at Piccadilly Circus. Near to the tube station, when the West Indies tour bus pulled up directly in front of us. For the twenty minutes in which it was parked there. We both stood speechless, and motionless. As though in a trance. As soon as it pulled away, we began talking excitedly between ourselves. That we'd seen the entire cricket team in person in their coach. We couldn't wait to get back to Amersham to tell all our friends about it. They couldn't believe it when we told them that we'd made no attempt to get any autographs.

My parents, youngest sister, Lois, thirteen, and eldest sister, Pam, twenty-four were on a three-week holiday to England. Based in Walthamstow, East London. Guests of family friends, Pam and Bads, and their two adorable toddler daughters. They'd toured all the London tourist attractions. Travelling to Amersham and High Wycombe, to see where I lived and worked. Joining cousins Marva, Carol, and Cynthia, who lived in the Birmingham area for a weekend. Driving to Lake Windermere in The Lake District. Staying overnight at a bed and breakfast hotel. Taking the opportunity on the following day to explore the other lakes, situated in the area.

Hermes's birthday was due soon. She was keen on celebrating it by hosting a party in the recreation room, alongside Chenies. We were required to obtain permission from The Personnel Department. They were reluctant to approve it, as a group of students had thrashed the facility, whilst holding a party there. "You won't have any problems with these girls." Countered Staff Nurse Bowen, as she happened to be in the department at the same time as we were.

On Friday the 20$^{th\,of}$ August 1976, I met Eddie at the party. He was a friend of Desmond's, who was a fellow student. He was accompanied by his friends, Lenny, Bert, and Junior. They'd arrived at 11P.M. Just as chicken curry, rice, coleslaws, and salad, prepared by me was about to be served.

Dressed in a pair of dark, blue jeans, and a light blue cheesecloth, midriff top. Eddie and I were introduced to each other. It wasn't long before he'd asked me to have a dance with him. By the end of the evening, he'd asked me for my telephone number.

The night sisters were supposed to ensure that all was in order. That the premises were vacated by 1A.M on the 21$^{st\,of}$ August. Our behaviour however was exemplary. No one came over to check. On the following day, Hermes and I cleaned the main hall, with accompanying kitchen, and toilets thoroughly. Handing over the keys on the Monday morning.

"Nurse Mottley, Sister Slater's room has been flooded!" Exclaimed Sister Tompkins, the night sister who'd come to the ward, to over-see me administering the patient's medication. "How did that happen?" I asked. Then I remembered that on that evening, after getting ready for work. I attempted to wash grapes in the sink in my room. After inserting the plug, I opened the tap. There was no water coming through. I'd forgotten to turn off the tap or unplug the stopper. I'd had to leave hurriedly for my night shift, to avoid being late on duty.

As I recalled what happened with Sister Tompkins. She filled me in with what had occurred. There was a problem with the water supply. It was being repaired. When everything had returned to normality, my sink had overflowed. Sister Slater's room flooded as a result, as her room was directly below mine.

I was often left in charge of the ward. Under the supervision of the night sister. Though not based on the ward itself, she covered the entire surgical unit. Ensuring each ward was run smoothly. Overseeing the administration of the medicine round, checking prescribed intra venous infusion bags, and analgesia for patients, following their operations.

It was a busy night, with six patients having had their procedures performed that day. My entire shift very much involved walking up and down the first three beds, on the left-and right-hand sides of the Nightingale ward. Regularly checking and recording temperature, pulse, blood pressure. Observing that there was no excessive wound bleeding. Indicative of shock. Ensuring that the urinary output was within normal limits. With the intravenous infusion running satisfactorily. Making sure that pain relief was adequate, and that the patient was comfortable. The toleration of having sips of water was essential to avoid having a dry mouth. It was important for each of the six newly post operative cases to be within easy reach of a call bell. To request any assistance when required.

Christmas was almost upon us once again. My grandmother, Auntie Oddie, Uncle Leroy, their four children, Trudy, Dion, Greer, Suzette, Great Uncle Allan, Great Aunt Thelma,(Tanti,)lived in Brooklyn, New York. I was intent on visiting them for the festive season, as I hadn't seen them since 1973. When my cousins and grandmother joined their parents there from Trinidad. My first Christmas away from home was spent with my mother's friend, Gwen Mabbs, and her daughter, Caroline.

Without any delay, I applied for a United States of America visitor's visa by post. Enclosing a letter of invitation from my aunt, and documents from the school of nursing and hospital regarding my training and employment there. As well as bank statements, proving that I was able to purchase my own flight tickets. Having the ability to look after myself whilst on holiday in Brooklyn.

The final allocation for my eighteen-month stint at Amersham, was twelve weeks. Eight on day duty, and four on nights on the geriatric unit. It was a busy department. Caring for confused, elderly, citizens, and for those with medical conditions, such as high blood pressure, diabetes, strokes, and respite care for carers needing a break.

Most of them were unable to bathe or wash themselves. Requiring help to do so. Some were bedridden, needing particular care with regular turning in bed. Ensuring that they received an adequate supply of fluids and help with feeding if required. One of the wards was responsible for the rehabilitation of those well enough to be discharged home.

The ward where I was working was managed by Sister Boyd, who was about fifty-five years old. Cheerful, happy, friendly, with bright blue eyes. Even when standing erect with her slender frame, and long blonde hair tied up in a bun, she wasn't much taller than the heavy, bulky, awkward, metal trolly, which was transported to the ward from the hospital's kitchen, by porters. This kept the patient's food at the required temperature.

There was also Charge Nurse Robinson, a fatherly figure, about sixty years old. Of medium height, with a few tuffs of silvery hair on his head, and an unusually firm abdomen for someone of his age group. "What would you like me to do Charge Nurse Robinson?" I asked him. "I don't want you to do anything. Just sit in the sitting room. I'm sure you've got some studying to do." He confirmed.

At my return from lunch. I first checked the workbook, indicating what duties I was expected to do for that part of the shift. My name wasn't included. On the previous afternoon, I was allocated to admit patients to the ward, of which there many. Including those for respite care. This kept me there until 6.30P.M. Charge Nurse Robinson had then returned from a unit meeting and was surprised that I was still on duty. He wasn't pleased that I wasn't relieved of my duties at 4.30 P.M. I drew enquiring glances from all the ward staff, as they buzzed around. He even offered me a cup of tea, and a piece of cake made by his wife.

I Will Survive

On Sunday the 26th of October 1976. I left my room for my early shift. Thinking it strange that there wasn't anyone around at Chenies, or in the staff car park. There was darkness all around me. I checked my watch once again. It was 07.40 hours. I was even more puzzled, when I arrived on the ward to see Sister Williams, the night sister doing the medicine round. "What are you doing here?" She enquired. "What am I doing here? I'm here for work. It's 07.40hours. Where's everyone?" I asked. "Don't you know that the clocks went back an hour at two A.M?" She questioned me. "Oh no I didn't. I didn't even watch the news last night when I got back to my room. I just had a bath and went straight to bed. No wonder there wasn't anyone around this morning. It's no point going back to my room. I'll make a cup of tea and relax with it in the sitting room." I answered. Throughout the shift, I became the butt of everyone's jokes. The best thing for me to do was to laugh along with them. That mistake was never again repeated. To make up for it I, I was sent home an hour early.

Having worked several shifts with Sister Boyd, and being supervised by her, for medicine rounds. All the time increasing in confidence. She encouraged me to conduct the procedure under examination conditions, with her being my assessor. Everything was running smoothly, until it was the turn of Mrs Smith. She was prescribed antibiotics for five days. I promptly read her prescription card. Noting the drug, date, and time. That it was given within the period required. Doing all this audibly enough, so that everyone was able to hear me. Somehow Sister Boyd insisted that I hadn't checked the validity of the tablet. I was referred by her for that reason. I accepted her decision with dignity. Not disclosing how upset and disappointed I really felt. Heading straight back to my room promptly after work. Remaining there until the following day.

It was mid-November 1976. I'd commenced night duty. I was often in charge of the ward, with the night sister available for support to conduct the medicine round. Quite often some patients would awaken in the early hours of the morning. Attempting to get dressed for work. There was also another who constantly shouted, "come to bed George." Tempting another to reply. "Shut up." It was imperative that we attempted to calm, and settle them, to avoid any confrontation amongst them.

My visa was declined. I needed to go to the U.S Embassy, in person, as soon as possible, to plead my case. Up and dressed at four A.M. The eerie, cold, damp darkness in the atmosphere was all around me, as I left my room. There was no one in sight as I boarded the bus, at the stop outside the hospital. My fingers numb and frozen, struggling to get the fare from my purse.

At Amersham-on–the-Hill, getting the underground train to Baker Street. This feeling of uneasiness persisted throughout my journey to Bond Street. Walking the last few yards to Grosvenor Square. There was a lack of heat in abundance around me. The crispiness in the air, and the plentiful supply of frost.

Armed with all the documents necessary to obtain my visa. I stood on the border of the embassy perimeter. First in the queue, at about 6.30A.M. With others quickly following, and lengthening it, within half an hour. Being first in the line of waiting people. I was attended to immediately the diplomatic building opened, about 8.30A.M. Showing the official all my evidence that I was able to support myself financially throughout my visit. An endorsement permitting travel was stamped in my passport, saying "requests two weeks visit to Brooklyn. May not work or study."

It was mid-December. Without hesitation, Hermes and I were given permission to host another party in the recreation room. Most of the afternoon was spent cooking, and preparing chicken curry, and rice, Cole-slaw, roasted chicken pieces, marinated with herbs and spices, and sandwiches. Carol, Hermes's sister, Rhonda, their cousin, and their friends. All Trinidadians. Students in and around London, and Eddie were amongst our guests. Once again, our behaviour was so impeccable that the night sisters never made an appearance.

On my final night shift before leaving for New York. I couldn't control my level of excitement. Longing for the period-of-time, in which I was at work to end. Rushing back to my room to have a bath, breakfast, and then head to Gatwick Airport, for my early evening flight to John. F. Kennedy Airport, New York.

On arriving there, I was bemusedly embarrassed to be handed a huge red card. Indicating that I was to be interviewed by immigration officials. On asking the reason, I was informed by them that it was because of the notice, "requests two weeks visit to Brooklyn. May not work or study," on my visa.

"I can speak English perfectly well thank you." A bureaucrat had begun speaking to me in Spanish. Maybe presuming that I was Puerto Rican. By this time, I was very tired and hungry. Suddenly, there was an explosion of frustration, and anger. "I've just completed a ten-hour shift, on a geriatric ward. Travelled hundreds of miles to the airport. Following a seven-hour flight, arrived at this airport. I'm exhausted! I'm a student nurse. I'm employed by my hospital, and the N.H.S. I receive a salary at the end of every month." Presenting to her all my documents.

"I've come here to rest and enjoy Christmas with my family. Why would I want to come here to work, and study, when I already do that in England?" Having examined my documents. Paying close attention to what I'd been saying to her. She said, "hope you enjoy your stay madam." With that my passport was duly stamped by her. I was free to collect my luggage, and to be met and greeted by my family.

The drive from John. F. Kennedy Airport in Queens, through to Brooklyn, was an enchanting, as if in a spell experience. From the rooftops above, to the gardens below of every building along the way. The Christmas decorations, obviously put up with care, love, planning and attention. Aglow and flickering with multi coloured lights. The combination of downfalls of snow energised the quality of light, emerging from the decorative bulbs. Allowing them to shine even brighter. Giving the scenery an even more fairy tale involvement. I was surprised to find that my cousins had grown so much since 1973. Trudy, the eldest was now fifteen. Suzette, the youngest was now eight. I found it impossible to keep my eyes opened for the first two days after my arrival.

There was an icy chill in the air. Auntie Oddie, Trudy, Dion, Greer, Suzette, and I were reluctant to again postpone another visit to Rockefeller Centre. We were at once freezing as soon as we'd left their warm home. Making our way to the subway. Getting the train to Manhattan. Once again, the bitter cold stung us. We stood amongst hundreds of people surrounding and admiring the tall, majestic Christmas tree, and all its beautiful lights. Falling victim to the weather conditions. Returning home much sooner than we would have liked.

January 1977 had quickly come, with the second half of my training beginning. It was a hard fall back down to earth following my holiday. Immediately returning to work on Ward 6A (female medical,) on the early shift, the day after my home coming. Fortunately, I'd moved all my belongings prior to my vacation.

The weekend cleaning book had disappeared. It couldn't be found anywhere. Mary Jones, another second-year student, and I exchanged glances. Not a word spoken between us. On the previous day's Friday-afternoon shift, she'd said in jest to me. A little twinkle in her hazel eyes. A huge mischievous grin on her face. Saying, "I don't feel like doing any weekend cleaning this week." Although we all assisted in looking for it, we were secretly thankful that it was missing. We all dreaded all those mundane tasks at the end of each week. To our relief there was no cleaning that Saturday and Sunday. On the Monday morning, there was the book, lying open on the ward office desk.

The sky was littered with pigeons. It appeared to me as though there were thousands of them, like a magnet, headed in my direction. I had visions of them all landing on my head. With my feet stuck to where I was seated in fear. The loudest, high-pitched sound broke free from my gaping mouth. Everyone in the vicinity, at once turned to stare at us. The birds had ignored me altogether. Flying way above my head. Disappearing into the distance.

Eddie and I had arranged to meet at The Odeon Cinema, Leicester Square, London. To see the film, "One flew over the cuckoo's nest." Arriving there early, we sat in the open square, in the spring sunshine, close to the movie theatre. Surrounded by trees, and flowers. Perched on one of the park benches chatting. I felt so ashamed of myself. We'd only seen each other twice since we met in August. My fear of Aves had developed over time. After watching The Alfred Hitchcock film, "Birds" years before.

My high school friend, Annlyn had sent me a 21st birthday present via another colleague, Christiana. Her sister, Glenda was also a student nurse at Central Middlesex Hospital. Waiting at the nurses' home for me were Glenda, and her friend, May, who was from St Lucia, also a student nurse there. Whilst we enjoyed a cup of tea in Glenda's room, Patricia and Marcia, ex pupils of my alma mater. St Francois Girls College. Made their entrance into her room. They'd just completed a two-week study period at the school of nursing. The air was suddenly filled with joyfulness, as we whooped with delight. We hadn't seen each other since we left school. I ended up going along with them to a party, hosted by fellow Trinidadians later that evening. Not returning to High Wycombe until the following afternoon.

Integrated within the hospital, was the Outpatient's Department, providing outpatient care. Based there for four weeks, my job was to chaperone patients into consultation rooms, to be assessed by medical and nursing staff. Providing support and advice, as necessary. As well as conducting tests, such as blood pressure, urine, weight, height, measurements, or any other requests made by the relevant professional.

Next came two months working with Sister Godfrey, District Nursing Sister, who organised nursing care in the community in Marlow. A town within the Wycombe District, on the river Thames. Four miles south of High Wycombe. Our days were spent visiting patients in their homes. Giving wound care, catheter care, support with taking medication. Working with G. P's, preventing unnecessary hospital admissions. Sister Godfrey and I enjoyed a good working relationship. I was eager to learn, interacting well with patients, and work colleagues. She, and her husband took me to lunch on our last working day together.

I'd overslept. It was 11.30A.M. I was supposed to be meeting Eddie at one P.M, at Claybury Hospital club house. He played in the hospital's cricket team, against other teams in the area. The cricketers were already on the field of play. Eddie was bowling the over. There sitting amongst a few rows of chairs, in front of the club house, overlooking the field, were Kitts, from Trinidad, and Luretta, from Barbados. They were friends of Eddie's, and I sat alongside them. Even though we'd never met, we sat throughout the match, talking, and laughing as though we'd known each other our entire lives. Also being introduced to fellow cricketers. Steve, and his wife, Joan, and Richard.

The Mighty Sparrow, one of Trinidad and Tobago's famous calypsonians, was due to perform in High Wycombe. Hermes and I were thrilled to be going. We'd spoken about nothing else for weeks. In all our years growing up in Trinidad, we'd never been to any of his concerts. It was unbelievable that we'd come to High Wycombe to see and hear him sing. The hall was packed with people. The excitement at fever pitch. The music electric. Bringing the house down as soon as he began to sing "The Statue." His well-loved calypso of 1976.

My third and final year had begun. It was a ten-week stint on the gynaecology ward. During this time, I was successful in my nursing care assessment. I was intending to return to New York for my three-week summer holiday in July 1977. I didn't have the ideal opportunity to explore the sights of the city, as I would have liked, when I visited at Christmas. I was required to obtain a new visa. My previous one had expired. To my surprise, the permission for indefinite visa usage was stamped in my passport, for the document's duration.

Like seven months before. My grandmother held me closely in her arms. Lovingly greeting me with the words, "Darling are you hungry? Do you want something to eat?" There was a lot of love in and around her. And she gave of that freely to anyone and everyone.

The weather was in stark contrast to my last visit. The heat unbearable at times. I climbed all the way to the top of The Statue of Liberty. Witnessing the New York city blackout. Watching on television the crowning of the first black Miss Universe, Trinidad, and Tobago's Janelle Penny Commissiong.

What I most fondly remember, was my great aunt and uncle, each tightly holding my hands, as we crossed the busy road to attend the show at The Radio City Music Hall. Prompting me to say to them, "I'm 22 years old, and you're still holding my hands." In their eyes, I'd remained the little girl that existed not so long ago.

I'd heard about Sister Singh before I'd even started working on 6B. (Male Medical) She may have been of small stature, but what she was lacking in height, she more than made up with mental strength and character. Originally from Guyana. Always immaculately dressed. Without a hair out of place. A perfectionist at heart. Everything had to be faultless. Even the temperature charts had to be very neatly charted. Woe betides anyone who hadn't obliged. With blood pressure recordings in red, pulse in black, and temperature in blue.

"Richard Williams. Forty-five years old. Admitted to the ward with high blood pressure. Has commenced a twenty-four-hour urine collection for V.M.A this morning." Reported Sister Harris at staff handover. One of a group of five students busy writing on our notepads all the details. None of us knowing what V.M.A was, or even bothering to ask. "Nurse Mottley, what is V.M.A?" Sister Singh asked me." "I don't know Sister Singh." I answered. Her voice became louder, and crosser as she asked each student in turn the identical question. The answer remained the same. With a face and voice that portrayed the sound of thunder, came these words. "When you all return from your coffee break. I expect you all to know what V.M.A is." We all missed our break. Dashing instead to the pathology lab., enquiring all about twenty-four urine collections for V.M.A. Brimming with anticipation, and excitement on returning to the ward, knowing all about it. Disappointed that she never mentioned it.

Next working on 5A, (female surgical) with Sister Daniels being the senior ward sister. Originally from Trinidad. Of medium height, a sergeant-major type figure of authority, who preferred things in perfect order.

"Cross infection, Nurse Mottley!" came the resounding sound of her voice. I couldn't see her, when peeking out of the bay, which was situated next to the sluice. Attempting to rush there to put a patient's towel in the skip. Instead, I was scurrying back to Mrs Smith's bed side, to return her soiled towel. Then going back for the skip, so that the towel could be placed in it, at the foot of the patient's bed.

It was February 1978. I was due to sit for my hospital final exam soon. I hadn't done any more assessments since 1977. Remaining lacking in confidence since the mishap in 1976. By now, I should have completed all my practical exams, before taking the hospital finals in March, and the state final in June 1978. I'd worked many times with Mrs Hulme, (clinical tutor,) who was supporting and encouraging me to do these three tests. Aseptic Technique, drug administration, and ward management. Even though I was competent in performing these procedures. I was very anxious about working under examination conditions. After one morning of changing dressings, under aseptic technique, and the administration of medication, whilst doing the medicine round. I was incredibly surprised when she said to me. "Congratulations Nurse Mottley, you've passed." After much planning, preparation, and practice. I passed my ward management assessment. Where I was in charge of the ward, for the entire shift. With all four now under my belt. I was well and truly ready for both final examinations.

Once my hospital final was completed, and I was successful. I requested to work on 6A. (female medical) Also applying for midwifery training at Dartford Hospital. The results were out. They'd arrived by post that morning. Elisheba, Carol, and Priscah had opened their envelopes, with shouts of jubilation. Revealing that they had passed. With trembling hands, I attempted to open my letter. Hoping that this would not be a case of Deja vu. I've never passed an exam at the first attempt. At the third time of trying, the letter slid amongst my shaking fingers. I couldn't see the words, "I have the pleasure of informing you." Instead, "I regret to inform you," shot out at me, like an arrow, straight to my heart.

I felt cold, and shivery on the inside. My mouth dry. My lips glued together. Unable to utter not one word. Eventually, I gathered enough courage and compassion within me. Regaining my composure. Smiling warmly. Giving each of my friends a congratulatory hug. Then it began to sink in. My offer of midwifery training at Dartford was no longer viable. I was required to re-sit the exam in October 1978. Terri hadn't sat the exam with us in June. Therefore, Hermes, Terri, and I formed a study group. Holding discussions amongst ourselves at every opportunity. Mostly through the night. Having regular breaks. Listening to music, chatting, and eating.

It was 11.30P.M. My silhouette was wandering around in the darkness. Struggling to open the locked door to Grovelands. There was only the faint, visible light, coming from the moon. Someone had called the police. There was a squad car coming up the driveway. Somehow, I managed to open the door, escaping into the building. Just in time, to avoid any interaction with them. Returning to Hillview, where Terri lived, with a cake, chicken, and macaroni pie, which I'd retrieved from the oven, in the kitchen on the ground floor of Grovelands.

Keeping awake was proving to be exceedingly difficult. My head continued to fall forward. Then up again. Bending, and sagging like wilted flowers in the scorching mid-day heat of the sun. Priscah and I were passengers on the ferry. Crossing from Dover to Zeebrugge, Belgium. Both up at the crack of dawn. Preparing to board the coach from High Wycombe to Victoria Coach Station, London. Transferring to our holiday coach for the week's Three Capital's European tour. We were the only two people in our student nursing group, to be awarded a week's extra holiday. We hadn't used all our allocated sickness allowances during our three-year training.

What a relief it was when there was an announcement, towards the end of the four and a half hours journey, over the ship's tannoy. Preparing us for our departure from the vessel. It was almost midnight when we arrived at our hotel. Our home for the next two days. Up at 7A.M, with breakfast at 8A.M. We were all eager for our touring of the city. The capital of Belgium. Administrative centre of The E.U. Headquarters of NATO. Home to politicians and diplomats.

First to the cobbled square of the Grand Place. The central square of Brussels. The main tourist attraction. A market until November 1959. Surrounding it was the town hall, The King's house, and several houses built, and rebuilt over time. We visited Le Manneken Pis next. The small, bronze sculpture of a naked, little boy, urinating into a fountain's basin. Then unto The Atomium. An impressive, large, sturdy building. Initially made for the Brussel's 1958 world fair, celebrating the progress of science. Built of stainless-steel clad spheres, to form the shape of unit cells of an iron crystal. Situated at the front of Brussel's Park, in the centre of the city, was The Royal Palace of Brussels. The official palace of the Belgian monarchy. Not used for residential purposes. The Royal Family live elsewhere in the city. On the other side of the park, was the Belgian Parliament building.

On our third morning, immediately after breakfast. We set off for Amsterdam. Arriving there some three and a half hours later. Seeing windmills, and beautiful flowers along the way. Yearning to get to our hotel, as soon as possible. To off load our luggage and have some lunch. To explore the city's artistic history, and famous canal system. Touring via our coach, as well as by canal cruise. Seeing Anne Frank's house, where she and her family hid during world-war two. Visiting the Van Moppes diamond factory. Famous for the purchase of sparkling engagement, and wedding rings. Lying in splendour in their little boxes, in a secure environment. Buying samples of Edam cheese, whilst visiting their cheese factories. Also purchasing souvenirs of clogs at the clog factory.

Driving through the red-light district. Then to the Dutch town of Volendam, to the northeast of Amsterdam. Famous for its colourful, wooden houses, and old fishing boats lying in the harbour. Priscah and I were surprised to find that the film, "Saturday Night Fever" was the premier attraction at the cinema near our hotel. We took the opportunity to watch it, as we never had the chance in High Wycombe. We couldn't believe that we'd travelled all the way to Amsterdam to see it.

Dinner by candlelight in a French restaurant, whetting our appetites for a Paris by night coach tour. Paris, famously known as the city of light. The first to use gas street lighting. A city well known for art, fashion, food, customs, and way of life. The magnificent Eiffel Tower. The wrought iron, lattice structure. All lit up, in all its splendour! Visible for miles around. Leading all the way up to the heavens. Of similar build to London's Marble Arch, is the Arc de Triomphe. A celebrated memorial to those soldiers who fought and died for France.

On the 56th floor of the Tour De Montparnasse is a restaurant and terrace, requiring a rapid experience of a lift ride to get there. Open to the public, it conveys very impressive views of the area. The Avenue Champs-Elysees, lying near where the Arc de Triomphe is situated. Renowned for its theatres, boutiques, and luxury shops. The cafes with numerous amounts of people sitting outside. Amongst the trees lining the wide street. Enjoying and appreciating the cuisine. The habitual practises and way of life of the French. It is also the finishing line of the Tour De La France Bike race. A few days later making our way back to London Victoria Coach Station. Driving through the French countryside. Passing through the battlefields of both world wars. Unto Calais, to board the ferry to Dover.

Terri, Hermes, and I had just completed our exam paper. A feeling of immense joy came over us. Pent up energy released, and flowing up to its surface, like an erupted volcano. Emotionally, freedom felt huge, and we intended to celebrate the occasion. That evening, venturing out into Uxbridge. In the suburbs of Middlesex, bordering the county of Buckinghamshire. The recently released thriller "Wild Geese" was showing there.

Six weeks later, our results were due. I was at work. Terri and Hermes were off duty. They were supposed to telephone me as soon as the postman had arrived. I hadn't received any calls or messages from them. It was already11A.M. I couldn't keep still. I'd become distracted and was unable to concentrate. Understanding how I felt, Sister Bell sent me for my coffee break, advising me to take the rest of the day off, as she believed the postal worker, would have arrived by the time I'd returned to the nurses' home.

Mrs Hulme entered the dining room as I'd sat to have my drink. She immediately made her way over to me to congratulate me. A huge smile on her face. The school of nursing had already received our results. She was taken aback that I hadn't been aware of my success.

Joining the other two waiting outside Grovelands for the mail carrier's arrival. Running towards him, as he made his way up the driveway. Even though I knew that I'd passed, it didn't spoil the awesomeness of the occasion. That evening, the three of us, and several of our friends gathered in Terri's room. Where we'd always met for our study group. It was in an area of Hillview, where there were many vacant rooms. We needed that peacefulness, as we revised during the early hours of the morning. So as not to disturb anyone. As increasingly more of our friends appeared. The food, drink, and music really began to flow. Terri's bed was banished to the corridor outside her room.

Arriving at Barking Hospital's Maternity Unit. With ample time for my interview, for the 29th of January 1979 intake of midwifery students. I was surprised to find that the lovely lady with the pleasant, cheerful voice, who I'd spoken to yesterday, about the advert in The Nursing Times, was the Director of Midwifery, and the person who was appraising me. I was travelling to Brooklyn within the next few days. Returning on the 15th of January 1979.There and then, I was measured for my uniforms. Undertook a medical examination, and received a letter for the home office, and immigration authorities. Regarding my offer of employment, and training. Eddie was also moving to Preston, Lancashire, on the 28th of December, to commence psychiatric nurse RMN training at Whittingham Hospital, Goosnargh, Preston. There wasn't enough time for us to visit each other before our separate departures. Further apart from each other now, more than we ever were.

Chapter Five

"How am I going to fit into my nurses' uniform?" I wondered. As I climbed into the back seat of the taxi taking me to Amersham. My overnight flight from New York had landed at Heathrow Airport. With there being too much luggage in tow, to facilitate travel on the trains and buses, to get me there. Where I was registered to work with a nurse agency. Until it was time to begin midwifery training on Monday the 29th of January 1979.

My grandmother took great delight in encouraging me and everyone else, to do nothing but eat. "You need fattening up." She told me. One morning I'd come downstairs to the kitchen for breakfast. I was quite taken aback by the sight of the postman sitting at the table. Enjoying a hearty meal of bacon, scrambled eggs, tomatoes, mushrooms, toast, and a cup of coffee. She admonished him for not having had anything to eat before leaving home for work.

The Christmas and New Year season involved visiting family and friends. Not wanting to appear ill mannered was unthinkable. Having to eat whatever I was offered. As a result, none of my clothing would fit. Therefore, I'd landed at the airport dressed in my aunt's attire.

On the Friday morning prior to my start date. I moved with all my belongings, which had been in storage at Wycombe General Hospital's Groveland's Nurses' Home, Barking Hospital, Essex. With the help of Lillian, a removal van, and it's driver. Lillian was like a mother to me, since I met her in the lift at Chenies nurses' home, when I moved there in July 1975. With Umilta, Pat, Sybil, and Grace, like aunts. Providing stability, and support for Hermes and me, like a family would. During our first three years in England.

The driver was eager to complete his return journey promptly. Therefore, it was left to me to finish the move. Making several trips to my room on the first floor. Carol De La Motte, my next-door neighbour, who'd moved on the same day as I did, and I were yearning for a cup of tea, before we began to unpack our things. Carol also twenty-three, originally from Sri Lanka, had recently qualified as a State Registered Nurse. Relocating from Brighton, Sussex.

At 9A.M on Monday the 29th of January, our intake , all dressed in our nurses' uniforms. Carol, Elizabeth, Terri, Anne, Suzanne, Bernie, NG,Dora, Barbara, Monica,(a nun and state registered nurse, training to work as a missionary midwife in Africa,) and I, were gathered in the classroom of the school of midwifery, on the ground floor of Barking Hospital maternity unit. Our tutor was Mrs Harris. Of medium height, rather plump, but a motherly figure to us. She often spoke of her daughter, a similar age to us. Our consultant obstetrician lecturer, Mr White. Probably in his mid-fifties, with balding, receding white hair.

It was a twelve-month course with Barking Hospital assigned to be the health facility, where the first sixteen weeks of training took place. The first week was spent in the classroom. Learning the rudiments of the art of being a midwife. Each Monday was selected to be our study day, in the classroom, which we were required to attend in our uniforms. Each tutor giving us assignments, and projects, to be completed at a required time.

There was a letter addressed to me via the school of midwifery, from Eddie, on my desk in the lecture room, on the last day of our study week. A quiver of joy flooded through my body as soon as I'd seen it. Not having enough time in which to read it. I quickly put it in my handbag, to study its contents later at my coffee break. As the morning's classes were about to begin. The mid-morning recess couldn't come soon enough. It had been posted from Preston, Lancashire, a few days earlier. Giving me details of his new address, and telephone number. Asking me to contact him as soon as possible. I hadn't seen or had any contact with him in over two months. As I digested the letter's contents, the relief from hearing from him once again was comforting. Dispelling the thoughts that I'd never see him again.

There were three wards on the unit. Shaw, Read, and Williams. With each of the consultants responsible for each one. Consisting of ante natal, post-natal, and labour segments. With Read having the obstetric theatre for the unit. On Monday the 5th of February 1979, I began my first shift on Shaw Ward. Where each morning there would be rows of urine samples, lying in the sluice. Ready to be tested for any abnormalities. There would also be several twenty-four-hour urine bottles to be assessed for oestriols. Hormones made during pregnancy, which determines foetal health, and well-being, to be transferred to the pathology lab.

The new experience of palpating the differing shapes and sizes of the expanding pregnant uterus. In addition to listening to the foetal heart, with the aid of the Pinard stethoscope. Was a task that took me a while to accomplish to my own satisfaction. It was imperative that ten deliveries had to be witnessed before participating in any myself. With the patient's permission obtained beforehand. As it is such an emotional, and personal experience, and a privilege to be part of. Each normal birth observed, involved detailing it, in a booklet. Signed by the relevant professional.

"Mrs Brown's fully!" declared Staff Midwife Sheila Richards. As she carried a tray, loaded with mugs, a pot of tea, and some milk from the ward kitchen. Placing it on the desk of the ward office, situated next door to the kitchen. There was a patient on the ward called Mrs Brown who was in labour. Although not looking after her. I was awaiting confirmation that her baby was ready to be born. I had witnessed five normal deliveries and was desperate to achieve the magic number ten. Rushing past the office. Walking in the direction of her room. I heard Sheila's voice calling me. Changing direction, I entered the office to much laughter. I hadn't realised that "Mrs Brown's fully" was the universal password for midwives, with the secret message of tea is ready.

It was a cold winter, with a stockpile of snow. Hindering us from getting to work from the new nurses 'home to the maternity unit. Leaving us no alternative but to get there via an underground tunnel, which connected the maternity unit, and the general nursing departments of the hospital.

Very quickly I was aiming for the next step in order to qualify as a state certified midwife. With a midwife scrubbing up alongside me, to assist in the delivery of my first five babies. After having looked after them in labour, progressing to the safe arrival of their infants.

I'd admitted Susan Smart, who was accompanied by her husband, Robert. My morning's shift had only just begun. She was concentrating solely on breathing in. Taking deep breaths to help control the pain of her mild to fair contractions every four minutes. With each one becoming more painful than the last. In the throes of her first pregnancy of thirty-eight weeks. She said, "I've been up all night. Unable to sleep. Wearing the carpet thin by walking up and down on it. Having bath after bath, paracetamol after paracetamol."

On admission, her observations of temperature, pulse, blood pressure were within normal limits. On palpation her abdomen corresponded to her due dates. Longitudinal lie, Cephalic presentation, Engaged. Foetal heart heard regular, using a pinard stethoscope. Even before the procedure was completed. She was requesting to use Entonox. 50%oxygen, 50%nitrous oxide, as her first method of pain relief. Continuing to look after her during my shift, with half hourly checks of pulse, the length, strength, and frequency of contractions, with any accompanying vaginal loss. Foetal heart rate, and her ability to cope with the severity of the pain. On vaginal examination four hours after admission, her cervical dilatation had progressed to 6-7 centimetres. The foetal heart was beating regularly.

As the pain threshold of each contraction decreased. Her self-control and dignity began to disappear. The sweat poured across her furrowed brow. Also, down her clammy cheeks. Her eyes doubled in size, depicting the terror that was taking control over her entire body. Showing the magnitude of her distress. As fast as we comfortingly and soothingly wiped her face with a dampened cool cloth. The perspiration reappeared.

She cried and shouted out in agony, and despair. Grasping Robert's hand so tightly, that he himself was shrieking in anguish. Pleading with him, "help me, Robert! I need some Pethidine now!" As her hold of the end of his arm intensified, and the Pethidine that I'd just given her coursed through her body. It produced its desired effects. She began to rest, and even sleep in between her contractions, as the tension drained away from her body. At 4.00P.M, she had an uncontrollable urge to push, with no visibility of the head. At 4.40P.M the head was seen. Steady advancement of the presenting part, with strong contractions every two minutes. Foetal heart regular. 4.50P.M She was screaming, shouting, and crying with every contraction every two minutes, and using Entonox. I was due to finish my shift at 5P.M. Volunteering to remain behind, to support her, instead of handing over to someone else she wasn't familiar with. At 5.05 P.M, the foetal heart rate was decelerating without recovery. Medical aid was summoned. Leading to a Neville Barnes forceps Delivery of a live male infant. The ward's workload was hectic. There was no one to relieve me of my duties. It wasn't until 8P.M that I'd returned to my room.

I'd never been to Preston. I'd heard about the Lancashire town during my "O" Level English Literature classes. Reading the story of Sissy Jupe, and the other characters of the Charles Dickens novel "Hard Times." Depicting the lives of those working in the cotton mills there.

Off duty for the weekend. Immediately after breakfast, I'd set off from Upney to Euston via The London Underground. Climbing the stairwell to the mainline train station. Making use of my student railcard, to purchase my return train ticket. Waiting for about thirty minutes, before boarding the Intercity locomotive for the two-and-a-half-hour journey. The halfway point between London and Scotland. Travelling at speed through the English countryside. Admiring the differing scenery of the landscape. City life versus country life. The tranquil views of the various farm animals, and the greenery of the fields surrounding them.

As I alighted from the coach, unto the station platform. My wandering eyes failed to identify Eddie. Then I felt these strong, comforting arms around my waist. Drawing me closer towards him. We hugged and kissed each other, unmindful of the other people around us. Enjoying a leisurely ten-minute walk along Fishergate. Strolling up to Preston Bus Station. All the way talking about what had been taking place in our lives, since we'd last seen each other. We caught the Ribble bus heading for Whittingham Hospital. In the village of Goosnargh. A parish of the town of Preston, Lancashire.

Situated between Broughton, and Longridge. A five–and-a-half mile journey there. Leaving behind the business and businesses of the town. A drive of about forty minutes along Garstang Road. Observing the expansive lawns of Moor Park. The stateliness of the large buildings along the way. Passing through Fulwood, a small prosperous area to the north of Preston town centre. A part of the main town itself.

Very soon, we'd driven past the M 55 intersection, leading towards Blackpool. We'd entered Broughton. Another small village. The serenity and green pastures surrounding the village's parish church, elegantly standing a way back from the main road, along a narrow driveway, with a small graveyard prominently in position in front of it.

I Will Survive

At the corner of Garstang Road, and Whittingham Lane, were two pubs diagonally opposite each other. First, The Golden Ball, and then The Shuttleworth Arms, as we turned right into Whittingham Lane. A narrow country road, portraying large family homes, with long driveways leading up to them. Followed by farmland, heading towards the hospital.

Having entered the village of Goosnargh. The Stag's Head pub came into view, along with a few shops. As well as several family homes. Our bus then followed a sharp turn to the right. Turning right a few yards ahead. Entering the psychiatric hospital's extensive well cared for grounds. With large buildings built during the Victorian era. Stopping at the bus stop, just inside the gates.

Across the small road, lined by trees, and a cricket field on the one side, and a car park on the other, was a large building comprising of wards, and nurses' accommodation. Walking along a corridor of limited width, we approached some stairs, which led to his room on the floor above. Once there, I immediately flopped with sheer exhaustion, unto an armchair, lying next to his bed. Enjoying and entwining my cold fingers around a hot mug of tea. This he'd handed to me before disappearing into the kitchen to prepare a meal for us. Before our departure for the Friday evening's disco at the hospital's sports and social club. The drubbing of the beats coming from the sound recording system, could be heard even before we entered the building. Dancing and enjoying the music until it was almost midnight. My departure back to London on the Sunday afternoon, took hours on the slow locomotive. Stopping at every station back to Euston.

Bernie and Staff Midwife Shaw had barely left for their break to the comfort of the ward sitting room, as the clock struck midnight. The shrillness of the buzzer disturbed the peace and solitude of the hour. It was the last night of our two-week stint on night duty. Our quietest during this period, in the run up to Easter. With all the babies due then, already delivered.

"I feel like pushing, nurse!" Mrs Johnstone cried out. With a voice full of pain and fear, as I entered her room. "Push?" I asked her in disbelief. I'd seen her only a few minutes before. She was fast asleep in bed then. She was 37 weeks pregnant. Admitted for rest and observations for the treatment of high blood pressure. The baby's head was advancing quickly, as she drew her legs up towards her chest. Clasping her hands around her legs. Making deep grunting noises, originating in her throat. Attempting to force her baby through the birth canal. I'd immediately summoned help by pressing the emergency call bell. The night duty sister, Sister James, arrived on the scene promptly. Just in time to witness the birth of a baby girl. The remainder of the shift passed uneventfully. With us leaving the ward on time.

It was the 13th of April 1979. Good Friday morning. I'd planned to visit Lillian for the Easter weekend. Setting off from Upney Lane, about an hour after my shift ended. At Baker Street, the Metropolitan Line train, which I'd boarded was bound for Watford. I was due to change for the tube for Amersham at Harrow-on-the Hill. As I opened my eyes, I was surprised to find that there were two guards leaning over me. Shaking my shoulders, attempting to awaken me.

Back from Amersham, following the Easter break. It was back to day duty, where it was unusually quiet, after the mad rush of deliveries before the holiday began. There was no one in labour at that time. Making it the ideal opportunity for parentcraft sessions: Nappy changing, folding of terry nappies, advice on healthy eating, the importance of having adequate rest, baby bathing, top and tailing, help and support with breast feeding mothers, with assistance and encouragement for mothers, in the sterilisation of feeding bottles, and in the making up of feeds.

I continued to sneakily glance at the ward clock. Every minute, it seemed. From 4.20P.M onwards. Hoping that I'd be able to make a rapid get away at 4.30P.M. As soon as my early shift was completed. It was Friday afternoon. Rush hour time. My ambition. To get to St Pancras mainline station by 6P.M. To catch the train to Leicester.

Since January 1979, Terri was a student midwife at Leicester Royal Infirmary. Hermes had also commenced midwifery training in Croydon in March. We were all getting together for the weekend. My fears were confirmed. As soon as the underground train began getting nearer to the city. With passengers sitting or standing, closer and closer together. Like sardines, tightly packed in a tin. Arriving at my destination promptly at 6P.M, for a 6.10P.M departure. When it was announced that there was a delay for our service, people became disgruntled. It didn't pull away from its buffers, until almost 7P.M. Rolling into the station at Leicester one hour and twenty-five minutes later. There to meet me on the platform, were Terri, Hermes, and Arlene, who was from Grenada. And in the same student midwife group as Terri.

Back at the block of flats reserved for midwives was Glenda, originally from Guyana. Another one of Terri's class-mates. The apartments were spacious, and comfortable, with three bedrooms, one for each of the girls. Kitchen/ diner, sitting room, bathroom, and toilet. Our weekend involved sight-seeing, as Hermes and I had never been there before. Shopping, visits to the cinema, and disco. With time spent together enjoying each other's company.

The last month of the first sixteen weeks, was spent on the ante natal clinic. Chaperoning pregnant women in and out of consulting rooms. To be examined by obstetricians and midwives. Observing their weight, testing their urine, and checking their blood pressure for any abnormalities. Palpating their abdomens, ensuring that the foetus was growing satisfactorily. Listening to the foetal heart rates. That they were beating regularly, and steadily. Noting whether their babies were moving well in utero. Providing help and support, as necessary. Assigned to work with Mr Wright, our group's consultant obstetrician lecturer. In one of his ante natal clinics one Friday morning. We provided care to an unaccompanied Spanish woman, in her early twenties, whose command of the English Language was poor. Suddenly, incredibly grateful for my "O" Level school girl Spanish. I was able to step in as a competent interpreter.

In order to progress to our next stage of training. A twelve–week care in the community programme. We were required to be successful in a written and oral examination. After which we all enjoyed a two-week holiday. I visited Eddie again. During this time, realising that our long-distance relationship was impossible. With the depth of studying, and work commitment involved.

Chapter Six

Arriving back at Barking Hospital following my two-week break. Refreshed after visiting Lillian in Amersham, and Umilta, and Pat in High Wycombe. I moved once again to the student midwife community wing, on the first floor of the Old Nurses' Home, along with the other students in my group. Our uniforms remained the same, but now with the addition of a navy-blue community coat and hat.

Allocated to work with community midwifery sisters from either Barking, or Redbridge. I was assigned to Sister Cotter. Based in the Ilford/Seven Kings areas of Redbridge. Mondays remained our study day. With lectures held in the community in the town hall in Ilford. On our first working day, Sister Cotter, a very pleasant, happy, middle-aged, motherly, community midwife, whom I felt incredibly at ease with. Met me in front of the Old Nurses' Home. Thereafter, we'd arrange to meet in Ilford town centre. From whence, we'd make home visits, whilst travelling in her car. Visiting newly delivered mothers, and babies. Ensuring and checking each mother's uterus was firm, and well contracted, her lochia (vaginal loss after birth) was normal, and the perineum (the area between the anus and genital organs) and/or stitches were comfortable, clean, and healing.

That pain relief was adequate. That the mother was having enough rest, and support at home, and was eating healthily. Providing help and assistance for any problems encountered. Observing whether the baby was feeding well. Weighing the infant regularly. Noting any changes in stool appearances. Making sure that the cord stump was cleaned with a sterile swab at each visit. Leaving an adequate supply of them for the mother to cleanse, as necessary. Watching for any signs of psychological jaundice.

I Will Survive

Our group was able to bond better now that we were all together in our unit. Having our own spacious, well-equipped kitchen. Lovely bathroom suite, with shower rooms, and hair drying facilities. Our own sitting room, and a room for storing our equipment: delivery, ante and post natal packs, swabs, cotton wool balls. Cord clamps, ligatures, syringes, and needles. There was a depositing box for used instruments to be sent to C.S.S.D for sterilising. We also had our own phone, enabling contact with community midwives, and other agencies. I was nominated as the best deserving occupant of the biggest room. Slightly larger than a double bedroom, as I had so many things in my possession.

On Saturday the 23rd of June 1979. The West Indies and England cricket teams played against each other in the final of the second cricket world cup. Glued to the television set in my room. Watching the West Indies team bat first, losing early wickets. Then Viv Richards, Collis King, and the tail enders scored 286 for 9. In reply, The English only scored 194. The West Indies had won their second world cup. Prompting me to jump up and down in celebration in my room and along the corridor outside it.

Anne and Suzanne were commemorating their twenty first birthdays, in our sitting room, at a surprise party, which we'd orgasnised for them. They'd known each other since they were children in Ireland. They were also best friends. Carol and I did the cooking. Chicken curry, and rice, Trinidad, and Sri Lankan style. With further international flavours, supplied by NG, from Malaysia, with Chinese delicacies! Wantons, and spring rolls. Our group was indeed the United Nations, with Bernie, also Irish. Dora, Ghanian. Liz, Monica, Terri, and Barbara, English. It was great that we all got on so well together.

We all made ante natal visits too. Checking and recording the mother's blood pressure, testing their urine for any abnormalities. Performing abdominal palpations, inspecting, and registering that the size of the abdomen, and the presenting part of the foetus, corresponded to the expected date of delivery. Listening to their baby's heart-beat. Observing that it occurred at regular intervals. Enquiring of the mother, whether their baby was moving well. Most of all, listening to, and advising them on any problems they encountered.

Three weeks had passed, my assistance hadn't been required, whenever I'd been on call for the evening. I'd only just returned to my room, having been working at the G.P clinic with Sister Cotter. It was an extremely hot and humid summer's day. I'd become sweaty and uncomfortable. My hair plastered to my head. Deciding to have a shower to relieve myself of this uneasy feeling. I was in the shower cubicle with my eyes shut. The shampoo running all over my hair, face, and body. Liz ran into the bathroom, saying in a steady high-pitched voice. "Helen, you've got to be ready in ten minutes. The taxi's picking you up to take you to Ilford Maternity. There's a G.P bed patient in labour." Liz was holding my bleep whilst I was in the bathroom. "I haven't had anything to eat yet." I declared. Quickly getting out of the room and getting dressed in my uniform. Luckily my hair was almost dried, as I rushed through the the front door of the Old Nurses' Home. Jumping into the back seat of the car, to meet the community midwife at the hospital. Being greeted and presented by Anne, Suzanne, and Liz, with a hot meal on my return a few hours later.

On a mid–August Sunday morning, I visited Priscah, who now lived and was a student midwife in Margate. A south-eastern English town on the Kent coast. Enjoying most of the rides on the amusement park. Venturing into Broadstairs to see the Charles Dickens Museum. Having a meal whilst we were there. Rushing back to Margate train station for the journey back to London Victoria. It was a Sunday service scenic route rail journey, stopping at every station along the way.

On return to London, I'd run unto the District Line platform to Upney almost at the stroke of Eleven, as the last train took its leave. I couldn't believe it. How was I going to get back to Barking? The taxi queue was rather lengthy, as I inched closer and closer to the top of the line. "Please can you take me to Barking?" I asked the taxi driver. Pleading with him, "please you've got to take me to Barking Hospital, Old Nurses' Home. I missed the last train to Upney. I'm a student midwife there, and I'm on duty in the morning." Without hesitation he said, "hop in." It was one "o'clock in the morning when I opened the door to my room.

At 6A.M, there was a gentle knock at my door. It was Suzanne, who was on call. She was almost whispering, "Helen are you awake? There's a patient booked for home delivery, who's in labour. I've already had a few home births. Would you like this one?" She asked me. I was the only one in our group who hadn't had any. On being offered the opportunity, I jumped at the chance. "The taxi will be here in fifteen minutes to take you to Dorothy Winchester in South Woodford." She told me.

Being greeted by Dorothy's mother on arrival, very much reminded me of my grandmother. "Have you had any breakfast?" She asked me. Grandma was there to look after her two-year-old granddaughter, and to support her daughter. She had made me a very welcoming cup of tea, and two slices of toast with bacon. Community midwifery Sister Williams was already in attendance. I'd arrived to look after Dorothy, under her guidance and supervision. The atmosphere was so relaxed. Much more than being in a hospital. Her toddler running into her bedroom, whenever she wanted to see her mother. At eleven "O" clock that morning, I delivered her second baby daughter. 7lbs 4ozs.

I distinctly heard the words "white horse" coming from behind me. I briefly turned around to see who was speaking. To my surprise, it was Lilly. I hadn't seen her since she left Amersham several years before. She was now a health visitor in Ilford. I was on my way to the baby clinic at the church hall. Using my push bike, given to us, at the start of our twelve-week programme. A form of transport to attend baby clinics, and midwifery lectures in the community. As we gained experience working with our district midwives. Towards the end of our three-month period, we became involved in conducting our own home visits. Reporting back to our mentors.

Another get together in Leicester was organised for Hermes, Terri, Gail, Maryam, and me. All students together in High Wycombe and Amersham. There was a knock on my room door. It was my parents, Cecil and Dearest, and two of my sisters. Pat,26, and younger sibling, Lois, 15. They were on a two-week holiday in England. And had come to spend the day with me.

Carol De La Motte had previously applied to work as a staff nurse in Australia. Her application was finally successful. She'd decided to curtail the rest of her midwifery training, in order to follow her heart. I saw her off at Upney Lane Station and was sorry to see her go.

At the beginning of our community care programme. We were divided into sub-groups. With each team given a project to complete, and to be presented at the end of the course of study. Ours was entitled, "care of the under-fives in the community." It was a nerve-racking experience for

Monica and me to present it. However, it was well received by our tutors and classmates. We were immensely proud to have done such a commendable job.

On our last working day together. Sister Cotter took me out to lunch. I was incredibly grateful to her for being such a kind, thoughtful, understanding, and patient person. Someone on whom I could always rely. She'd done her best to teach me all that she knew about the community midwife , and care in the community.

Chapter Seven

The nights were gradually closing in It was September 1979. The third term of our midwifery training had begun. Our group had all moved to the nurses' home, Ilford Maternity Hospital, Newbury Park, Ilford, Essex, for a period of sixteen weeks. Built in 1926. It was otherwise known as The West Wing of King George Hospital. With the latter lying alongside the maternity unit.

Our study day was now on a Thursday. Held in the classroom on the ground floor, towards the back of the nurses' home. Our studies now concentrated on the abnormal aspects of midwifery. Making my way from the nurses' home, situated at the front of the hospital. Walking towards a small building, directly behind it. Which housed Elizabeth Fry, (ground floor) ante natal/labour ward, and Marie Curie, (first floor) post-natal ward. It was a much smaller unit than Barking's. And because of that, it had a more homely atmosphere.

My first allocation was to Elizabeth Fry, day duty. As I entered the ward, directly on my right were two rooms. Containing eight ante natal beds. On my right was an en suite toilet/ bath admission room. Where ante natal mothers were admitted to the unit. The nursery was located on my second right. Towards the middle of the ward, stood a wooden staircase, leading to the first-floor ward. Next to the staircase was the ward kitchen. The first stage of labour, delivery rooms, and sister's office brought up the rear.

On duty were Sister Matthews, in the early stages of her first pregnancy. Staff Midwife Greenwood, a midwife of two years. Staff Midwife Smithson, newly qualified, and two students, Terri, and me. We were introduced to one of the nursing officers in charge of the unit. Mrs Sheehan, who appeared to be in her mid-fifties, and very friendly in welcoming us to the unit. She was conducting her ward rounds of the hospital. Making sure all was well within the unit.

In the first ante natal room, were two patients. Mrs Smith, admitted with high blood pressure, and Mrs Forshaw, with reduced foetal movements. There was no one in labour, but there were to be two inductions that morning. Waiting in the sluice for Terri and me were two urine samples, ready to be tested, and blood pressure and foetal heart monitoring's to be checked for any abnormalities. Rachael Thompson. 28 years old. Had arrived accompanied by her husband, Chris. Crying and in a lot of pain. I gently guided her into the admission room, so that I could admit her to the ward. Whilst reassuring her that all would be well.

She was 38 weeks pregnant, and this was her first pregnancy. After taking her observations of temperature, pulse, blood pressure, and urine sample, which were within normal limits. I confirmed on palpation that she was 38 weeks gestation but was unsure of the nature of the presenting part. This appeared to be breech. The foetal heart was heard and regular. On vaginal examination, her cervix was four centimetres dilated, and a soft presenting part was felt. The foetal heart was heard using the Pinard's stethoscope. Requiring confirmation of my findings. I requested advice from Sister Matthews, who verified that it was a breech presentation. Promptly the doctors attended, explaining to her that her baby needed to be delivered by emergency L.S.C.S. As it was a safer way in which to give birth.

The consent form was signed. Blood samples were taken for full blood count, and group and save, should any complications arise, requiring a blood transfusion. An I.V.I was set up. An anaesthetist visited, informing her all about the anaesthetic she was about to be given. Confirming the timing of her last meal. I began to prepare her for theatre. Ensuring that she was wearing an identity bracelet. That the details written on it were correct. Giving her Mist Mag Trisilicate to drink. In order to prevent any harmful effects should she inhale any of her stomach contents during the procedure. I changed her clothing to a theatre gown and cap. Removing her jewellery and nail varnish. She didn't have any dentures, crowns, or caps. Shaving her vulval and lower abdominal region. Passing a catheter into her bladder, to avoid it becoming distended during the operation.

She remained uneasy. Her hands shaking like a leaf. Her lips quivering, as I accompanied her to theatre. Clinging to Chris's hand as he reassuringly held hers. Repeatedly we both assured her that she was going to be O.K. and that her baby's heart-beat was fine. Handing over her care to the theatre staff.

Three weeks later, a scene of utter chaos greeted us. Two staff midwives, and two students. As we arrived on duty for the night shift, on Elizabeth Fry. It sounded as though a horror film was being made there. The sounds of loud, piercing, pleading shouts and cries. Escaping and resounding from the labour ward. Creeping down the corridor. And out into the outside world.

There were two patients in the final phases of the first stage of labour. Allocated to look after Laura Greenwood. A 25-year-old primigravida. Admitted in spontaneous parturition at 38 weeks. She was completely deaf. Having contractions every three minutes and was seven centimetres dilated. Sent for my break at 11.30P.M. There was my home cooked meal waiting for me as I arrived in the hall. Adjacent to Elizabeth Fry. Amanda Greenwood was given the responsibility of making sure that all staff were promptly eating, so that they'd have enough time to be nourished by food and drink. Before having to rush back to work if required. I was then called back to deliver Laura of a 7lb. 3oz boy.

Following the week's night duty. I began working on Edith Cavell Ward. A much smaller unit of single rooms mainly for specialist post operative L.S.C.S care. And those specifically hospitalised for bed rest. Needing close monitoring. For example, Preeclampsia, high blood pressure, gestational diabetes.

Autumn was in full progress during my four weeks working on Special care baby unit, at Barking Hospital. As Ilford Maternity didn't have specialist facilities for neonates. Hospital transport was provided to get us there. Sometimes driving through thick fog on the early morning and late evening shifts.

The Special Care Baby Unit particularizes in the care of ill babies. Some developing infections requiring intra venous antibiotics. Treatment of babies of diabetic mothers. Jaundiced infants, and premature or low birth weight new-borns. In my care, on the low dependency area of the unit, was Timothy Jones. He was delivered normally four days previously.

Was initially nursed on the ward. However, his serum bilirubin levels were increasing. He was being looked after lying naked. His eyes protected from the bright lights of the overhead phototherapy unit above him. In an incubator, keeping him warm. This encouraged the bilirubin in his blood to be broken down by the liver.

His mother Anne seemed unsure of how to manage him, and his unwillingness to feed. To enhance bonding and confidence in taking care of her baby. I showed, supported, and encouraged her in caring for her infant as much as possible. To not be afraid of all the equipment. Explaining its usage to her. Providing advice and help in showing her how to stroke his cheeks gently to encourage sucking. Reassuring her that his condition would improve with the treatment provided.

However, his blood levels increased to such a dangerous degree, that an exchange transfusion was necessary. This was caused by the build-up of bilirubin in his blood. As babies have a lot of red cells in their bodies, which are being broken down and replaced constantly. At the start of my afternoon/evening shift, the procedure commenced. A lifesaving process, as his blood was slowly removed from his body. Replaced with fresh donor blood.

After a few weeks gaining expertise within the low dependency area. I began working on the high dependency unit. Helping to look after premature babies, or those requiring assistance with their breathing. At regular intervals, as on each ward. There were frequent teaching sessions. Held between students, midwifery tutors, and ward staff.

Then it was back to Ilford. Providing post-natal care, support, and advice on Marie Curie Ward. Observing, and recording each mother's temperature, pulse, blood pressure. Whether the uterus was returning to its normal position within the body. Noting and recording the output and colour of any vaginal loss. Paying close attention to any swelling or bruising of the legs. Encouraging a good diet and sleeping pattern as much as possible. Giving as much help and support as required with feeding their babies. Providing parent craft sessions, such as baby bathing, top and tailing, nappy changing, sterilising feeding bottles, and making up feeds. Post-natal exercises were promoted, especially those for the pelvic floor, helping bladder function. Some jaundiced babies were cared for on the ward. In incubators/phototherapy units alongside their mothers. My last

I Will Survive

few weeks at Ilford was at the ante natal clinic. Moving back to Barking in early December 1979. The written exam held in our classroom. Our oral test at the Central Midwives Board headquarters in Gloucester Road, London. The Central Midwives Board was responsible for the registration, training, and regulation practises of midwives.

"Are these for Christmas or next Christmas?" The post Mistress asked me with a chuckle, as I posted my Christmas cards on Christmas Eve morning. I was full of a cold at that time, and hadn't been at work for the past week. Struggling to write my exam paper. My condition hadn't improved much a month later at the viva. I received a grilling from my three examiners. This filled me with dread. Mrs Harris had warned us that in the event of this happening. Our written paper wouldn't have been well received.

With my midwifery training now completed. I'd chosen to work at Ilford Maternity Hospital. My results were due that morning. I was eagerly awaiting the arrival of the postman. A gust of wind causing the door of the nurses' home to slam shut signalled his arrival. Pouncing on him like a swarm of bees around honey. The envelope felt thin. As though there was absolutely nothing in it. I'd failed! This was no surprise really as I'd had a terrible cold throughout December and January.

"Should I go back to work, or should I hide in my room or run away somewhere?" I asked myself. "No!" I thought. "I'm going back to the ward with my head held high. There's nothing to be ashamed about. I'll pass it next time." With dignity I returned, telling colleagues what had happened. Graciously congratulating all those who were successful. Feeling increasingly at peace with myself as I did so. The 11th of February 1980 couldn't come quickly enough. I was booked to go to Trinidad for two weeks for carnival.

"Helen! Where've you been? So nice to hear from you at long last." Eddie's voice appeared to sing with the joy of hearing my voice again, after all those months of no contact. "I didn't pass my exam. The resits are in March/April, and I'm going home for carnival." I told him. "Aren't you coming to see me before you go?" He enquired. "I'm off this weekend." He spoke. "I'm off this weekend too." I replied.

In intense nervous anticipation. We were approaching Piarco International Airport, Port of Spain Trinidad, shortly after passing the five islands in the Gulf of Paria. The aircraft's speed had gradually diminished.

Now flying at a snail's pace over the Queen's Park Savannah. I was strapped into my seat with my face almost stuck to the window. Pointing out each landmark on my journey there. I was home at last!

There to meet me at the arrival hall were my sister Pat, Auntie Oddie and Uncle Leroy. They'd come in from New York a few days before I had. It was a very blissful time. Visiting family and friends. Going to Maracas Beach. Eating bake and shark. Spending a day in Tobago. Visiting Lillian, my friend from Amersham who was also on holiday in Trinidad. Attending the Sunday morning church service with my family. Visiting my school friends. Observing the vibrancy and colourful costumes on display by the dancing parading bands. Accompanied by calypso/soca music on moving trucks, tempting, and awakening further joy in them. Witnessing first-hand the uniqueness of the spontaneity of Trinidadians. As I stood in a queue at the bank, waiting to be served. We were all listening to calypso/ soca music coming from the local radio stations. When a catchy tune began to play. All at once, everyone began singing and dancing. Returning to what they were doing as the music stopped.

Not forgetting my studies. My midwifery textbooks came with me on holiday. I allocated enough time daily in preparation for my exams. My heart once again felt as though it was being split into two, as I boarded the aircraft, on the 25th of February to return to London.

Short staffed on Read Ward at Barking Hospital. I was asked to work on the late shift there. I met Monica Augustine. A student nurse on her obstetric placement. She was also from Trinidad, living in the nurses' home at St Georges Hospital Ilford.

My eyes lit up and sparkled like a Christmas tree. As soon as I'd seen my examination paper, sat in the classroom at Ilford. As a smile of thanksgiving and relief spread across my face. Each question was based on topics that I'd most recently revised. I felt unusually at ease. Feeling quite pleased with my effort. A teaching session with Mrs Harris held a few days later. Judging from the answers I'd given her, led me to believe that I'd completed an excellent paper.

My oral exam in April, at the CMB headquarters in London yielded a much different reception this time. My three examiners seemed eager to meet me. Rising to shake my hand. Telling me what an outstanding paper I'd written. We hardly spoke about any midwifery topics. Chatting about West Indies/ England cricket, and the outfit I was wearing. Everyone had received their results apart from me. There weren't any letters for me when the postal delivery was made. I became very restless and unsettled. Anxiously walking up and down the labour ward corridor. I contacted Mrs Harris and the C.M.B. I was informed that my result was posted to me at the Nurses' Home, Ilford Maternity Hospital. That there was no alternative but to wait for the correspondence to arrive. Given the rest of the day off. I set off for Preston as previously arranged.

On my return. There was a letter waiting for me, as I opened the door to my room. I picked up the envelope. Noting that its contents made it quite thick. Probably indicating that I was successful. My hands began to slightly shake as I opened my mail. As I removed its contents, the first few words I saw were "I have great pleasure." I then realised that several of my friends and colleagues were gathered around my doorway. All waiting to congratulate me.

Chapter Eight

It was the end of November 1980. I was to commence an eighteen month post graduate psychiatric nursing course at Claybury Hospital, Woodford Bridge, Woodford Green, Essex. A huge mental health facility built during the Victorian era. Snuggled almost at the top of a hill. Surrounded by acres, and acres of land. Green fields, gardens, ponds, and many buildings. So, characteristic of those erected during that historical period.

After working as a staff midwife for six months at Ilford Maternity Hospital. I was moving to another nurses' home. It was the first structure on the left from the hospital's main entrance. Amongst trees, and well-kept lawns. There was also an inclusion of a bus stop, towards the front of the dwelling. From which the number 275 bus stopped to take passengers from Barkingside to Walthamstow, and vice versa.

The sturdy elegant looking three storey construction housed several female members of staff. With Cassandra and Juliette, originally from St Vincent, there to show me the ropes. Cassandra and I lived on the ground floor, where there was the availability of a large kitchen for our usage. Including the distribution of drawers, and refrigerator space. I wasn't the only one who'd chosen to clean my own room. Not using the domestic services provided to do so. Almost everyone on the ground floor was already doing theirs.

On the following Monday morning. I walked to the School of Nursing, which was behind the nurses' home and car park. The first two weeks of the programme was spent in the classroom. Introducing the four of us, Moira, Mary, Sue, and me, all State Registered Nurses, to psychiatry and psychiatric nursing. Our tutors were Mrs Elzing, Mr Austin Seed, Mr Luton King, and Mr Mike Cock.

From thence being allocated to Ward E3. My first ward, and the first of three long stay assignments. Accommodation was provided there for female patients, with long term mental illness. Some of whom fell pregnant whilst unmarried. Having children during the earlier part of the twentieth century, when out of wedlock was frowned upon by society.

The pace of activity being much more relaxed than what I was accustomed to, with general nursing and midwifery. Mainly supervising the women awakening. Getting washed and dressed. Having breakfast. Ensuring that they'd taken their medication as prescribed by the doctor. At six monthly intervals each of them, would be examined by the ward physician. With their blood evaluated for any abnormalities.

Some of them attended work at the hospital's Occupational Therapy Department. Making benches, stools, picture frames, and other handicraft. To those remaining, there were other activities, such as baking. Accompanying them to the Campbell Centre, where there was a café, selling tea, coffee, soft drinks, cakes, sandwiches, other snacks, cigarettes, newspapers. There was also a room available for listening to music. Another where films were viewed by patients and staff alike. Where disco's, parties, and clubs for the over 60's were held. In the evenings, overseeing the various daily procedures practised at the end of the day.

Eddie and I continued to see each other, but more regularly now. In fact, every other weekend. When he'd travel to London, or I'd visit him in Preston, by courtesy of my student railcard and British Rail. Whilst in London, we'd go to see friends Richard and Claudette Bynoe, a lovely couple who lived in Barking, along with their three-year-old son, Richard. A delightful, intelligent little boy, who'd told his mother that he wanted to marry me, and that we'd live in his Wendy house.

At the beginning of February 1981, I began working on the first of my three short stay admission allocations. With each one representing a certain catchment area. Providing the candidates for each ward. Those short stay assignations were in fact admission wards, for those allowed to enter voluntarily, or involuntarily, under the mental health act of 1959.

Once again watching over their activities of daily living. Making sure that they'd taken their medication as prescribed by the doctor. Encouraging those with a poor appetite to enjoy their food once again. Being part of ward meetings. Discussing each patient's progress. Seeing to it that each of them was assessed regularly by the doctor, and their blood assessed for any abnormalities, which could have been caused by their treatment.

There was involvement in group, and individual psychotherapy sessions. Interacting with them by engaging in conversations with them. Listening and enjoying music together. Playing games like Scrabble or table tennis. I particularly enjoyed the cooking sessions, including the shopping for the required culinary items. Attending disco's at the Campbell Centre. Promoting healthy activities by walking in the beautiful, extensive grounds of the hospital. This stimulated the release of endorphins. The body's feel good factor. Elevating the mood and self-confidence.

A sparkling bright, red Ferrari pulled up in front of me at the bus stop, near Walthamstow market. It was a cold, windy afternoon, as I stood there. Shivering and stamping my feet on the pavement. In order to keep myself warm, surrounded by several shopping bags. "Would you like a lift?" asked this pleasant, attractive, nicely made up, dark skinned young woman. Very smartly dressed in a two-piece black suit. As she rolled down her car window. I almost didn't recognise her. Then I realised that it was Martha, who'd been discharged from the admission ward I'd been working on. Seeing me hesitate. She said, "Come on. Jump in. You must be freezing! I'll give you a ride to the hospital." "Thank You Martha. How are you?" I asked, as I fastened my seatbelt. "Very well thank you. I'm back to work. Taking my tablets as I should do. Keeping fit. Eating healthily, and I hope to keep it that way." She replied.

Martha and I had built up quite a rapport during her brief stay on the ward. After becoming depressed following her grandmother's death. We were of a similar age. Having the same interests, such as music. It was great that she was doing well, and back to work as a solicitor.

"You're not concentrating!" said Michael. Michael was one of our patients, working in the Occupational Therapy Department. "We've got a good thing going..." The radio was switched on. I couldn't resist singing and dancing along to the beats of the song. Now working in the department, making stools. With the four legs of it being wooden. Having to weave this plastic, straw-like, synthetic material. In my chosen colours of green, red, and yellow, to the top of my product. Judging by the amount of nagging and prompting used. I believe Michael, James, and David were secretly having a competition, to see which of their students would complete their masterpieces first.

The department also created activities such as picture framing, and pottery. My attempt at creating a vase, was rather pitiful. The clay wildly spinning, and disintegrating. Some of it flying all around the room. This served the purpose of helping patients to be part of, and cope with daily living. Occupational therapists were also part of the rehabilitation and admission wards' teams. Helping, and supporting them to manage their everyday lives, with activities such as doing laundry, cooking, budgeting, improving work skills. Enabling them to lead independent lives.

I then became part of the community psychiatric team. With various community psychiatric nurses, attached to different catchment areas. Gaining experience in each region. Visiting individuals in their home settings. Making sure that they were following their prescription requirements, as prescribed by their doctors.

Also attending clinics in G.P surgeries. Whereby progress was monitored, whether they were coping with life, or if any help could be offered. At these clinics, Modecate injections for the treatment of mental illness, such as schizophrenia, was given at a maintenance dose, once treated orally. The injection being slowly released into the body. It was therefore especially important that physical examinations, including blood tests, were carried out at regular intervals to detect any abnormalities.

"Coz, we got love times love." Eddie was in London for the weekend. We were visiting his friends Ernie and Rosa. As the music filled the air with the George Benson classic. We joined in unison. It was then that I realised that Eddie was indeed truthful. I'd never seen such a collection of music by anyone anywhere. There was an entire room with numerous shelves. Dedicated to the storage of record compilation.

What a joy it was to see my sister Pat in Brooklyn, New York in June/July 1981. She'd arrived there two weeks before I did. We spent time together shopping, visiting friends and family. Enjoying a day trip to Great Adventures. A large amusement park in New Jersey with our cousins. My two high school friends Maureen, who lived in Trinidad, and Diane, a dental student, living and studying in the U.S, visited me at my aunt's home. With Pat's departure, came the appearance of Eddie for two weeks. With the opportunity for us to meet with each other's families. As I returned to

London, my eldest sister, Pam, landed in the Big Apple, providing Eddie with the chance to become acquainted with her.

I was looking after seventy-nine-year-old, Harry Campbell. At the E.C.T clinic that morning. He'd become depressed following his wife's death a few years earlier. Checking that he'd had a chest x ray, and ECG, which assesses heart rhythms and electrical activity as it beats, that he had given his consent for the procedure, and that he'd nothing to eat or drink for six hours prior to his treatment. Equipment monitoring his blood pressure, pulse, oxygen levels, were attached to his arm, hand, and finger. And an EEG, tracing his brain action were all connected to the appropriate body parts. In readiness to be utilised as he fitted.

The anaesthetist proceeded to give him his anaesthetic, including a muscle relaxant, and oxygen. Once he was asleep, and fully relaxed, his treatment was given by the doctor. An electric current was passed through his brain to produce an epileptic fit. In order to relieve his symptoms. As the effects of the muscle relaxant wore off, leading to his awakening. He was transferred to the recovery area. I continued to assess his vital signs at regular intervals. Once being recovered, offering him a cup of tea, before transfer to his ward.

At the day's end of the middle of a two-week study period at the school of nursing. I could hear the telephone at the front entrance of the nurses' home ringing madly. As I approached it. There was no apparent attempt to answer it. Flinging open the back door. I quickened my footsteps to get to it before it stopped ringing. It was Eddie with the news that Claudette had given birth to a baby girl, Karen.

Now working on Ward C3. Dealing with the challenges of mental illness in the elderly. Managing conditions such as depression, arthritis, and epilepsy. On which it was important that each patient was familiarised with the layout of the ward environment on admission. So that they would feel secure. Maintaining their own independence. It was assessed by the medical, and nursing staff, physiotherapists, and other members of the ward team, whether any help was required with any problems in their daily lives. Attentively listening to their concerns. Enjoying, and interacting with them with social activities. The support of occupational therapists and physiotherapists essential for them to relearn the skills required to care for themselves. To maintain their self-sufficiency, using lists to improve memories. Exercises to relieve body pain and stiffness, with medication and treatment plans used as required. Family support becoming especially important, with the possibility of changes to the home to ensure safety.

Awoken by the loud, shrilly, sounds of fire engines, racing up the driveway of Claybury Hospital, with all guns blazing, to the car park at the rear of the building. Hearing the deafening noises from the firemen's boots, as they rushed up the stairs, to the upper floor of our building. Accompanied by the clamour of the fire alarm system. It didn't take me long to get out of bed. Quickly wrapping my dressing gown around me. Hurrying outside my room, to find out what was happening. All the other girls on my floor were already there. Standing in a group in the corridor.

The roof of the dwelling was deluged with water by snow, over the past few days. Ensuing to burst pipes on the upper floor. Where there was water everywhere. The home warden was already on site. It was1. 30A.M when the entire building was required by the firefighters to be evacuated, as it had become unsafe.

It was exhausting trudging through the many inches of snow. Dressed in my pyjamas, dressing gown, boots, and covered in blankets, to protect us from the elements of that wintry night. We were given shelter at various nurses' living quarters throughout the hospital. Once the offer was depleted, Cassandra, Debbie, Sita, Vindra, and I were grateful to be accommodated on the beds available at the E.C.T clinic. Providing an element of surprise for the staff arriving for the start of the 7A.M shift.

Karen's christening party was in full swing, with everyone enjoying themselves, when it ended abruptly. The women at the celebration were insistent that they weren't going to miss any of the gripping episodes of Dallas. Immediately the music stopped once JR was shot. The frivolity at once ended, with a stillness that surrounded the entire room, as all the guests began to disappear.

As I returned from work, there was a letter from Mrs Elzing waiting for me, under my door. Pat was getting married on the 6th of March 1982 in Trinidad. My study programme didn't allow me any time to be present for the occasion. To my delight, I was free to attend the wedding. Grabbing my jacket and handbag, I rushed out to the bus stop. Getting the double-decker to the travel agents in Barkingside. Splitting my R3 rehabilitation ward allocation, was the only way in which I could attend the nuptials. R3 prepared patients for discharge into their own communities. With the skills required to enable them to look after themselves as responsible adults.

Steve's grandmother was returning to Barbados following a two-month holiday to London. As luck would have it. We were booked on the same British Airways flight. Providing me with transport to Heathrow Airport. Steve was a charge nurse on one of the admission wards. We sat together on the aeroplane for the nine-hour journey to Bridgetown. The aircraft practically emptying for the hour's travel to Port of Spain. My cousins, Ken, Margaret, and Wendy had touched down on their flight from Toronto at a similar time as mine. My father eagerly waiting to greet us.

The bright, sunny, and cheerful day made a perfect back drop for the day's event. Attended by family and friends from America, Canada, England, and The Caribbean, providing the ideal opportunity for us to reconnect with each other. Not forgetting meeting up again with school friends and spending a few days in Tobago.

I'd just finished my evening shift on R3 and was walking alongside a small group of other nurses going back to the nurses' home. When I heard the most distressing news. Steve had died. How could that be? I'd only seen him a week ago, and he appeared to be in good health. As I approached the telephone in the hallway. I decided to call Eddie to let him know what had happened. They'd been friends for such a long time. As shocked as I was. He told me that he intended to contact Richard for any further information. Joan, Steve's wife, also from Barbados, and a ward sister on one of the admission wards. Was taking his body there for burial. There was to be a memorial service to be held in the hospital chapel, so that everyone would be able to pay their respects.

Once again, I'd failed my state final exam taken in June 1982.In order to gain my registered mental nurse qualification. My parents Cecil, and Dearest, and brother Skippy were on holiday in England in July/ August 1982. Visiting friends in Manchester, before returning to Seven Kings, where I was now living with Joan, and her superb toddler son, Christopher, supporting her at this challenging time.

Eddie was driving from Preston to Seven Kings to meet my parents. Arriving there earlier than expected. Probably feeling a bit anxious about being introduced to them. I was hoping that my edginess wouldn't affect him. Having had a rather strict upbringing. Experiencing first-hand my

I Will Survive

father's reactions to my older sisters' boyfriends. It wasn't something that I was looking forward to.

Once I'd introduced them to each other, and we'd sat down to our Sunday lunch. The uneasy emotions continued. My father sat quietly at the dinner table. Before making his excuses. Disappearing upstairs as he'd finished his meal. Eddie and I continued with our plans for me to relocate to Preston. I applied for a full-time staff midwife day duty post at Preston Infirmary. Delighted to receive a reply from Mrs Thompson, Nursing Officer Day Duty, to attend for an interview in mid-October 1982. Seeing that I'd come from afar, she'd arranged for me to have my medical and to be measured for my uniforms on the same afternoon. Following a successful interview.

Richard, Claudette, and their two beautiful children, Richard, five, and Karen, fifteen months, left London for St Philip, Barbados in November 1982. Joan and Christopher, almost two, joined them there shortly afterwards.

In early December1982. I learned that I'd passed my repeat examination. I was now qualified as a registered mental nurse. In the week before Christmas 1982, I visited an ex-midwife colleague of mine, Elizabeth Goh, who was returning to Malaysia. Before I moved to the nurses' home, Preston Infirmary, Deepdale Road, Preston. To commence my job as a staff midwife day duty on Monday the 3rd of January 1983.

Chapter Nine

Our friends Desmond, Lyn, Charles, and Pat, from London, were celebrating with us new year's eve 1982, at the party held at Whittingham Hospital Sports and Social Club. Two days later, on Monday the 3rd of January 1983, it was my first day at work on the maternity unit at Preston Infirmary. A new chapter in my life was just beginning, as a small amount of self-doubt crossed my mind.

Smartly dressed in my new uniform. Consisting of a dark blue/grey nurses dress, with a white buttoned on collar. Red elasticated belt. A white nurses' cap, with a reversable navy blue/red nurses'cape, wrapped around the full length of my clothing. Black tights, and black well-polished leather shoes on my feet, ready to begin my early shift. Firmly placing my hand on the door-knob. Opening the door to my room. Reassuringly thinking, "well, I've done this so many times before. There's no need to worry. I'll be o.k." This appeared to work, as I immediately began to feel less anxious. Joining a small group of midwives making their way across to the maternity unit.

This Georgian building reminded me so much of Ilford Maternity nurses' home. Even though each building was from a different era in British history, they both extolled so much character and excellence in the way they were erected and built. Briskly walking down, the dark brown Jacobean wooden staircase. Deciding to make use of the underground passageway, of usage during world-war two, which led to the maternity unit, as the morning was quite cold and blustery.

Met by Mrs Thompson, Nursing Officer, day duty, outside her office on the ground floor of the building. Warmly greeting her three newest members of staff. Assigning Mary to the ground floor, ante-natal ward, Angela, to the Labour ward on the first tier, and me to the post-natal ward,

I Will Survive

also on the first level. The unit, comprising of three storeys, was situated on the right, immediately after the large, gated entrance to the hospital. Four elegantly portrayed stone columns at its approach. The ground floor accommodated Mrs Thompson's office, the ante-natal clinic, and pre-natal ward. The first housed the post-natal ward, the special care baby unit, and the labour ward. The G.P unit, and the school of midwifery occupied the second.

Introduced to Sisters' Baxter and Howard, staff midwives Inkley, Wilson, and Haston, and auxiliary nurse Higham, who made me feel very welcome. Learning new language terms of the northwest of England, "brew" (tea) and "butties" (sandwiches) quickly. Entitled to one week's holiday before the financial year began in April. I returned to London towards the end of March. Surprising Monica and Hermes with the news that I was expecting a baby in October 1983. I'd visited my G.P, receiving an appointment with the booking clinic at Sharoe Green Hospital maternity unit. I felt embarrassed about being pregnant. Having only just moved to Preston. Starting my new job, then taking maternity leave during the popular summer holiday season. The fact that I was unmarried played heavily on my mind.

Eddie and I had already begun looking for property in the area. Finally deciding on purchasing a three bedroomed semi-detached house in Fulwood, Preston. Moving there on the16th of May 1983. Life suddenly became very tiring, with exhaustion becoming my best friend. My work colleagues were amazing. Ensuring that I did no lifting. Being allocated to light duties only. Having lunch in the dining room over at the nurses' home. Immediately falling asleep in one of the comfortable armchairs in the sitting room next door. Then it was back to work, where all the mothers, and babies, were encouraged to rest. With the curtains drawn for about an hour before afternoon visiting began. I was made to rest as well. Sitting at ease in the nursery, during this peaceful hour.

"Can we help you?" asked two women. Obviously, a mother and daughter, as they mirrored each other's appearances, at the varying stages of their lives. We were walking from Sainsbury's Supermarket, towards the direction of the bus station. "You shouldn't be lifting!" The older woman advised me, with a look of concern on her face. "I'm only going to the taxi rank just around the corner." I told them, as they took my four bags away from me. Never leaving my side until I was safely seated in the vehicle.

It was the beginning of June. With my 28th birthday due later that month. Even though we'd made wedding plans for the next few years. Our baby's arrival in October, turned everything on its head. We'd decided to bring it forward to Saturday the 2nd of July 1983. Even though I was twenty-eight. I was petrified of telling my parents of my latest life events. That I was pregnant, with the baby due in October, and my imminent marriage plans. Eddie's and my parents first introduction hadn't gone according to plan. I couldn't face speaking to them. Only plucking up the courage to send them a letter of invitation, which arrived a few days before the event.

It was to be a small registry office wedding. With the reception to be held at our home. Following the purchase of our property, money management became more difficult. The booking of photographers was out of the question. Planning instead to engage our friends with the honour of this activity, in the beautiful grounds of Avenham Park. The cake was to be made by Pat's sister, who lived in Oldham. I'd planned to do the catering myself, but Hermes, Monica, Vera, and her daughter Shivaughn, helped in the provision of an efficient, professional, service.

With parental leave commencing from the end of July, the 28th week of gestation, until six weeks following the birth. We'd become inundated with visitors. Charles, Pat, and Monica from London. With a day in the Lake District with Ian and Monika. A letter from the home office had arrived granting me indefinite leave to remain in the United Kingdom. Relinquishing the necessity of applying for an annual visa.

Standing at the checkout at Morrison's Supermarket, about to pay for our shopping. I began to feel the trickling of something warm, and wet down my legs. Returning home as soon as we could. Making our way to the maternity unit. My labour had begun with the spontaneous rupture of membranes, and contractions every three to four minutes. The afternoon drew into the evening. The eventide into the night-time hours when the help of a Syntocinon Infusion was required to speed up my contractions. My confinement wasn't progressing as it should. Eddie had been sent home by the midwife during this uneventful time, so he could get some sleep. He never heard our telephone ring when the hospital switchboard tried to continuously contact him when his presence was required at the birth.

Edward was born at 0645 that morning, after I'd had my second injection of Pethidine. As with the first dosage, drowsiness and sleepiness encompassed my body. Hardly aware that Eddie had returned. I couldn't believe that I'd given birth to such a beautiful baby boy. So alert and inquisitive. Always eager to feed.

My terry nappies were frozen. There were droplets of water forming icicles on their surfaces. I was under the impression that they'd dry quickly, as the afternoon was incredibly windy. Hanging them on the line to blow dry, before taking Edward to the baby clinic. Life continued to be tiring, busy, and sleep deprived, during the first six weeks of his life. He was awake all night, sleeping more during the day. In order to help his non-stop crying, I put a dummy in his mouth. For a few seconds, there was a stillness in the room, as the sucking mechanism took effect. The screaming recommenced as soon as he realised that he wasn't being fed. Promptly turning his head to one side, spitting the dummy out in anger.

He lay in my arms, happily gurgling, as Mrs Thompson, and I sat in her office. Discussing the details of the reduction of my working hours. I was to be employed for twenty hours a week. Two mornings, and two evenings. Returning at the beginning of December to the ante-natal ward. Drumming up enough courage to telephone my parents. Informing them that they were grandparents to their new grandson, Edward. I was surprised to find that they'd seemed pleased about the news, happy to hear about his eagerness to perform all his milestones at an earlier stage of development.

On my first day back at work, I was welcomed with open arms by my work colleagues. Greeted with the words," lovely to have you back. How's Edward?" We'd enlisted the help of Jill, our child minder, who lived about a ten-minute walk from our home. Happy to fit in with the non-nine-to five-time scale, which we both worked. We planned all our working hours around his care, with any excess provided by Jill, who adored him as much as we did. He was alert, inquisitive, happy, and friendly. Already crawling, and in a hurry to walk and talk. It wasn't long before her mother, and other members of her family, were keen to meet him.

It was now 1984. Nothing could have prepared me for such a life changing experience as giving birth. Caring for someone so tiny, helpless, dependent on me twenty-four hours a day. As well as fitting in the requirements of housework, looking after a home, and going out to work. Edward had a curious, inquiring mind, from the second he was born. Crawling at ten days and climbing out of his pram before he was three months old.

There was a potent smell of coffee in the air, as Monica moved at ease from bed to bed. Offering patients their mid-morning cups of hot beverages. This caused me to breathe in deeply, to stop myself vomiting. I was again expecting another baby. Due in October.

Loud cheering broke the tense silence in the air, of the ante natal ward. All the patients and staff sat or stood around the solitary television. Their eyes transfixed on the screen. Portraying the finals of the winter Olympics in Sarajevo, Yugoslavia. On Tuesday, the 14th of February 1984, Torvill and Dean's spellbinding performance on the figure skating, ice dancing event also dazzled the judges. Announcing them gold medal winners.

The first test match between England and the West Indies, was being played at Edgbaston, Birmingham, from the 14th to the 18th of June. Eddie and I were on our way to London on the first morning of the game. We were listening carefully on what was unfolding on the field of play. As well as listening to music on our car radio. Happy that the English team were skittled out for 191 runs in the first innings. We were staying with Charles and Pat, visiting friends in and around London, Amersham, and High Wycombe.

"When is he coming again?" asked Jill's mother. After rushing over to Jill's house to see Edward, as I'd arrived to collect him. At eight months old, he was walking, talking, running, and attempting to pull her cat's tail.

I opened my front door to my cousin, Peter, his wife Carol, and their daughter Rebecca, who live in Canada, but were on holiday in the United Kingdom and Ireland. I hadn't seen him since he'd immigrated there twenty years previously. It was wonderful to see him again, and to meet Carol, and one of their daughters. With Edward and Rebecca playing together, whilst we caught up with family news. They were staying with us overnight, then on their travels again later the following day.

Our second son, Erle, put in his grand appearance in the early hours of the morning on the 17th of October 1984, at Sharoe Green Hospital's maternity unit. Returning home two days after his birth. Edward had gone for a nap and had awoken as Erle had settled down for a sleep in his pram. Not able to observe Erle asleep, Edward began to cry, until reassured that all was well, by seeing his brother sleeping peacefully.

I Will Survive

Why were they taking so long to arrive? Surely, they should have been here by now. My younger sister Lois and her fiancé, Brian, had landed at Gatwick Airport much earlier that day. Taking into consideration the length of time it takes to drive by coach. They should have been in Fulwood by now. As the clock struck eight that evening, there was a loud knock on the front door. They'd finally arrived. Delighted to see the boys. Edward, fifteen months, and Erle, three months. Dressed in their pyjamas.

It was superb that we were able to be together again since Pat's wedding two years before. It was almost Christmas day. The decorations were still in the loft. The minced fruit soaked in rum for the past six weeks, was begging to become part of a fruit cake. There was food shopping to be done, as well as a host of other things. We all worked tirelessly until the early hours of Christmas morning. Exhausted but happy to be together once again at one of the most family orientated of seasons.

Jill had moved to Garstang in September 1984, to be closer to her husband's new place of employment. She could no longer provide care for Edward, and now Erle. We'd acquired the services of another childminder, Margaret, who lived a few doors away from us. "Which would you like to hear first. The good or the bad news?" Eddie asked as soon as I'd returned home from my four-hour evening shift. "The good news." I replied. "The good news is that both boys are well and asleep. The bad news is that Margaret can't look after them anymore." "But why?" I asked. "She's not as flexible as Jill was. Finding it inconvenient to supervise their care before nine A.M, and after five P.M, and at weekends and bank holidays. She was under the impression that she'd have them for twenty hours a week. Not anticipating that she would be required for any less than that." He replied.

"When would you like to start?" Miss Wright, Nursing Officer Night Duty, asked me, as I was leaving for home one evening. "Is next week Monday and Tuesday, the 4th and 5th of March ok for you?" She enquired. "Thank you. That would be fine." I answered. As a result of our child-care providing difficulties. Sister Baxter, Mrs Thompson, Miss Wright, and I had decided that it would be ideal for me to work two nights a week. With my shifts rotating between the ante, post natal, and labour wards.

I'd arrived at Liverpool Lime Street station by train from Preston. It was Monday the 2nd of September 1985. My first visit to the city. I was due to check in at St Katherine's College, for my maiden midwifery refresher course, to be held there for the following five days. Unsure of where I should go to obtain my transport there, and with my stomach implying that I should get something to eat, as a matter of urgency. I found myself sitting in a nearby café, ordering tuna sandwiches, a side salad, and a cup of tea. I also asked the waitress directions to the bus stop. This resulted in a very pleasant drive of approximately twenty minutes through the outskirts of the city. Arriving at the spacious campus with delightful, extensive grounds, and solid red buildings, built in 1844. All in suitable time for the enrolment. All midwives in the U.K were required by law to participate in a refresher course every five years. Updating their midwifery knowledge, and skills, enabling them to practise as midwives. Also in attendance were my cousin Marva, and her friends Christine, and Elizabeth.

At the end of the second day, there was an optional session led by Anne Mortin. A Merseyside guide of Merseyside Tourism, who gave us a remarkably interesting talk, "Liverpool, city of surprises." Speaking about its history, places of interest, and most of all, its famous citizens. Cilla Black, and The Beatles. It was so well presented, and received, that she organised a sight-seeing tour for us.

Speaking to Eddie every evening, using the phone-booth on site. Reassuring me that all was well at home. My home coming was even more special, seeing their two little faces light up like Christmas trees as I stepped down from the train that Friday afternoon.

In March 1986, Preston Infirmary was closed. The buildings sold as residential homes and businesses. Our unit had amalgamated with the midwifery unit at Sharoe Green Hospital. Our joint services were transferred to a vacant four storey building on the premises. These once housed several general nursing wards, which had relocated to the newly built Royal Preston Hospital in 1983.

Chapter Ten

The drive from home to work was much shorter, since our move to Sharoe Green Hospital. A simple matter of approximately a five-minute journey, instead of twenty minutes. By-passing the old maternity wing at the entrance to the hospital, reaching the entry way to the unit. Being accessible via the lower ground floor, where there was a reception area, portraying a tiled image of a girl sitting on her bed, an opened book nearby, a cushion on her lap, holding up an object in her left hand, with a black cat on a green mat, attentively observing her. This had been brought over from Preston Infirmary.

There were also two gynaecology wards. One at either end of the building, and a gynaecology clinic. At each opposing entry to each ward, were lifts to the other floors. As well as a staircase, which fulfilled a similar effect. On the ground storey was M1. A twenty-eight bedded ante natal ward, on the right-hand side. With the ante natal clinic, and scan department on the left. Miss Wright`s, nursing officer night duty, and Mrs Rae`s, nursing officer day duty, shared office, was halfway between the two wards, and a corridor, linking the unit to the rest of the hospital.

Delivery Suite, and its sixteen rooms was situated on the first level, on the left. The Obstetric/Gynaecology theatre section of four operating rooms, the next-door neighbour. To the right were the G.P, and neonatal units. On the top tier were another two twenty-eight post-natal wards. M4, to the left, where the patients of Mr Wright/Manson, originating from Sharoe Green Hospital were admitted. M3, to the right, where patients of Mr Clarke/ Norburn of Preston Infirmary were permitted.

I was working two nights a week on wards M1, M3, M4, and Delivery Suite for two monthly periods at a time. The coming together as one of the two Preston maternity units, was no mean feat. However, it was a remarkable achievement. Requiring months of planning, staff meetings, and getting to know each other schemes. Inter unit exchanges of midwives for several shift patterns. The formal and eventual interaction at the end of March 1986. With the Infirmary night duty midwives, Veronica, Nora, Barbara, Maureen, Margaret, Madge, Kate, and I, and those of Sharoe Green, Winsome, Vivien, Heather, Dorothy, Pat, Sheila, and Margaret.

As the aeroplane landed at Grantly Adams Airport, Barbados. Edward at thirty months, was eager to stetch his legs, after such a long flight. As the doors of the cabin opened. An abundance of sunshine, and heat surrounded everyone on board. Edward ran squealing down the boarding steps as fast as he could. Shouting up to me," it's like being in the oven mummy." After an hour's refuelling and tidying of the aircraft, we were airborne once again. Landing forty-five minutes later at Piarco International Airport, Trinidad. Lois and Brian were getting married on Saturday the 31st of May 1986. Edward, and Erle, eighteen months, were accompanying me. Arriving several weeks before hand. Staying with my parents at Spring bank Avenue, Cascade.

It was a period of excitement. Helping with wedding preparations before the big day. The St Anne's Church of Scotland, Charlotte Street, Port of Spain, was vibrant with activity, colour, and heightened expectations. Greeting the advent of the bridal party. The guests, groom, and best man already seated in the church. Her face aglow with joy and happiness.

The gathering of relatives from Canada, The United States, and England, called for trips to Maracas Beach. While we pitched our position on the sand. My two boys quickly made friends with some people sitting nearby, having a picnic, offering them a chicken leg each. After our swim, enjoying delicious bake and shark purchased from one of the vendors along the plage. Annlyn, one of my closest school friends took me and the boys out several times. Whilst another, Marva, organized a get together at her home for Maureen, Ingrid, Roma, Marcia, and me.

The prospect of another plane ride excited the lads. This time for a week's trip to Tobago. Edward was in a rush to climb the steps to the aircraft. Landing there after a twenty-minute flight. Arlene, who I'd known since my childhood, and her husband, Fred, a secondary school teacher, and their two daughters, Jair, six-, and eighteen-month-old Jamella. They lived in Mount Grace. A very small village in Western Tobago, spending four days with them, visiting several beaches. Mount Irvine, a coastal village nearby. Lined with coconut trees, light brown sand, and turquoise waters. On our fifth morning, Aunties Thelma and Hettie, my mother's friends, arrived to take us to their home in Bethel, for the remaining three days.

It was very frustrating running from room to room in search of cardiotocograph monitor machines. As there were only two for the entire delivery suite. With swapping becoming a regular occurrence, resulting in complaints from midwives grabbing Mr Manson's attention. He commenced fund raising for the cost of supplying each room with the technology to monitor each mother, and foetus antenatally, throughout labour, and delivery. The cost of £250,000 was too much for the hospital's management to cover. Events such as The Krypton Factor style races, held at the army location, where the shows were televised. Pram pushes, football matches, played between midwives' vs doctors. Setting up a request for aid, "The baby beat appeal," with Sir Tom Finney being its first chairman.

"Careful the floor's wet!" came the shrill voice of the ward domestic, as Eddie opened the door leading from the dormitory into the ward sitting room, where he was employed as the ward charge nurse. Unaware that she'd mopped the floor, he'd hurt his lower back as a result and was unable to work.

We wanted to visit New York for a six-week holiday in March/ April 1988. Three weeks from the year April 1987 to March 1988, and three from April 1988 to March 1989. We were also required to obtain permission from hospital management, and to have booked almost a year in advance from when we'd intended to travel. Remaining on sick leave, Eddie continued to seek physiotherapy treatments for his back problem.

At last the 11th of March 1988 dawned. We were off to the Big Apple. However, the flight proved to be very uncomfortable for him. Having to sit throughout the seven-hour air travel from Manchester to JFK airport. We were staying two weeks with my father-in–law, Clarence. Two with Auntie Oddie, and another fourteen days with Lois, Brian, and three-month-old Brett in Texas. Flying from La Guardia to Houston, then changing aeroplanes for the onward journey to McAllen. All our neighbouring passengers and cabin crew becoming excited on hearing the boys' British accents, crowding around our seats. Engaging with them in conversation. Noting that our dialect was completely different.

Brian and Lois had recently moved to Mc Allen, where he now worked. A lovely, friendly border town, with pleasantly warm weather. Unlike the freezing, wintry, conditions we'd left behind in New York,where we met my sister Judy, her husband Gerrard, Tanti and three year old Jonathan. Our time there was enjoyable. Shopping, sightseeing, sampling Mexican food, and meeting my nephew Brett for the first time. Brian's mother Patricia visited us from Indiana, for the Easter holiday weekend. Driving across the border with all our necessary documents, to ensure a safe entry into Reynosa, Mexico. Exploring the area, shopping for souvenirs. Enjoying a Mexican meal in a restaurant. Travelling again into the Southern North American country, this time from Brownsville, another Texan town into Laredo.

The West Indies cricket team was touring England once again. During the summer months of 1988. The third test from the 30th of June to the 5th of July. Saturday the 2nd of July was the third day of the competition, and our fifth wedding anniversary. We'd booked tickets to attend the match on that day, along with Ian and Monika. Edward and Erle couldn't wait to see Gatting and Gooch bat for England. There was a tremendously congenial atmosphere at the match, amongst the fans of both teams who were sitting together.

Edward, almost five, was starting school at St Peter's C.E Primary School, close to our home. Just as Eddie, after having months of physiotherapy, was returning to work. With no relatives nearby. Having to share the responsibility of looking after the children ourselves. Working opposite shifts, Eddie on day duty, and I night duty. The person off duty taking and collecting children to and from school. It was a very tiring and demanding experience. Feeling desperately exhausted twenty-four hours a day. I would have greatly benefited from the help and support of family. However, I couldn't possibly have achieved much, without the unending love and assistance of Eddie, who was usually off duty whenever I worked. Helping to look after the home. Making sure that there was a meal on the table, for the boys returning from school. To be awoken by them, after being asleep all day, following a ten-hour night shift.

On my thirty-fourth birthday, at the twelfth week of my third pregnancy. There was a trickle of blood dripping down my legs, in the absence of any pain. Trying my best to remain calm, I telephoned my G.P, who advised me to make my way to G1 ward, at Sharoe Green Hospital. The bleeding continued throughout the afternoon, with increasing abdominal discomfort. Leading to the loss of my baby.

Erle started school in September 1989, at St Peters C of E Primary School, just as I'd discovered that I was once again pregnant, and due in April 1990. Unlike my two previous gravidities in 1983 and 1984, where the absence of work began at twenty-eight weeks gestation. It was now permissible to work beyond that. Up to thirty-four weeks. With the consent of the Occupational Health Doctor, who was required to review my condition on a weekly basis. On Tuesday the 27th of February, my maternity leave began. Our daughter, Natalie was born on Thursday the 26th of April 1990.Eddie again took two weeks holiday from work, to help, support, and look after me, and care for the boys, whilst I attended to the baby. The time permitted for returning to work, after the birth was extended from six weeks to six months. But this prolonged period was without pay. My second midwifery course was held in London in July 1990, at Froebel College, Roehampton, over the usual five days.

Wanting to spend the entire summer holiday with the children, settling the boys back into school, before returning to work in the autumn. I registered with a nursing agency in Preston. Working evening or night shifts in either Preston, Chorley, or Lytham, in a variety of nursing homes. At the end of October, I'd returned to my regular two nights at the maternity unit at Sharoe Green Hospital. A similar pattern existed as before. Where following my second night, Eddie would put Natalie to bed for an afternoon nap, before he left home for his late shift. We would then both awake at the same time, a few hours later.

Panting and out of breath, after running to the departure gate. I couldn't relax until we were all seated on the aeroplane. We'd somehow managed to get caught in a traffic jam to Heathrow Airport. Having travelled to London on the previous day. Getting there in the nick of time. There on the BWIA flight to Port of Spain, was my brother Skippy. A flight attendant with the airline. After months of planning, on notification that Skippy and Joanne were getting married on the 1st of December 1990. Gaining permission for special leave from school for both boys, and holiday arrangements for myself, and for us to be under Skippy's care during the flight, was something very special to experience.

As usual, there were family members from the U.S and Canada. Including Lois, who was pregnant with her second son, Rhys. There were the customary visits to Maracas Beach, Tobago, and catching up with friends. As all other family members returned to their respective households. We were spending the Christmas holiday in Cascade with my parents. Natalie and I attended a concert in downtown Port of Spain. With performances by a variety of steel bands, which we thoroughly enjoyed. Especially the dulcet, harmonious renditions of seasonal classics, which etched an occasion in my memory that I will never forget.

On Christmas evening, everyone gathered at my parent's home for our Christmas meal. As my brothers and sisters were having lunch with their individual families. During the entire time we were there, BBC news was inundated with talk about the invasion of Kuwait by Saddam Hussein since August 1990. The Arab nations were requesting support from the U.S and other Western countries. By this time, we'd safely returned to Preston on the 29th of December. In preparation for work on New Year's Eve, and for the boys to return to school early in the new year. Desperate to tell their friends about their vacation.

Chapter Eleven

There were government plans for Whittingham Hospital to be closed. Returning the patients into the community in Preston and other areas of the North-West of England. Eddie's ward had been shut, and he amongst other staff was responsible for placing them into the district residential setting. Suddenly, I awoke from sleep. Lying on the settee in my living room. Dressed in a pair of jeans, a t shirt, and cardigan. Without even casting an eye on the wall clock, to check the time of day. I jumped up, grabbed my jacket and car keys. Insistent that it was time to collect Natalie from nursery school. As I arrived there, I noticed that the children were outside playing. "Why are they outside, when they're supposed to be inside seated, all ready to be collected by their parents?" I asked myself, expressing my concerns aloud. I then realised that it was eleven O Clock, and not twelve O Clock. I was there an hour early.

After having worked a ten-hour night shift. I was operating on automatic pilot. Managing to get back home, and then to and from the nursery school safely. It wasn't until about 5.15, when Eddie returned from work, was I able to get to bed for a couple of hours before returning to work for another ten-hour shift. I may have looked a mess sometimes on taking her to nursery some mornings. Mrs Jones, the owner offered to bring her home, as she was required to drive past our home, on her way to fetch her son from school. Eddie's time in the Resettlement unit was now completed. He was now working in another department. In the care of those with Huntington's Disease.

I'd only just switched on my television set. The West Indies cricket team had lost two quick wickets, Simmons, and Williams. Brian Lara was walking out to the middle of the crease. It was the first morning of the fifth test at The Antigua Recreation Ground My heart was in my mouth, as the batters hit each ball. There was a steely determination in Lara's eyes and body language. Day by day his tally of runs increased. I was mesmerised. Fastened to my seat. Encouraging him on. At home everything revolved around it. Including meal preparation and times. At the start of the third morning, the excitement was tremendously high at the cricket ground. Sir Garfield Sobers was present at the ground. As well as television cameras from around the world. He was forty-six runs short of the record set by Sir Garfield Sobers in 1958, against Pakistan in Jamaica. As the scoring passed three-hundred and sixty-five. Sir Garfield Sobers made his way to the middle to offer his congratulations.

After waiting for the coach to arrive. We boarded the vehicle, settling into our seats, ready to be taken to the evening performance of "Joseph and the Amazing technicolour dream coat," at the Blackpool Opera House. Sue, one of the midwives on our unit had organized the all-round trip there. Including the tickets for the show for all the midwives, and their children, which we all completely enjoyed. Stopping off for fish and chips on the way back home.

My mother was spending two weeks holiday with us. Taking immense pleasure in taking Natalie to and from her reception class at school. Edward was now a member of the choir at Broughton Parish Church. Touring The Isle of Man, France, and visiting several churches, and cathedrals in England. As well as singing the Sunday services at their local church. In September 1994, shortly after their return from their French summer tour. They were giving an identical performance at St. Walburg's Church. A mid-19th century grade one listed catholic church, whilst my mother was still on vacation with us. She was so delighted with the singing that she stood ecstatically to attention. Both her hands grasped together at the start of Handel's "Hallelujah Chorus."

I woke up in agony. My left foot felt stiff, sore, painful, and difficult to move. Tentatively, I got up from bed, tired, and furiously yawning, due to the previous night, when I'd attended our night staff Christmas '94 dinner and disco, at The Bistro French Restaurant. The intention being that everyone was supposed to dance on the same cleared table that we'd just eaten on. Making way for others who'd climbed on for a group photo. I'd missed my footing. Stumbling off it, hurting my left ankle. Not realising that it was so painful until the following morning. What a struggle it was all day long. Unable to walk normally. Managing only to hop along on my left foot. I was supposed to be working that night as well!

It was hectic when I'd arrived on Delivery Suite. I was finding it exceedingly difficult to move around. Slowly hopping and hobbling from patient to patient, and from room to room. I must have been an incredibly determined person. To have accomplished the conducting of my duties over the ten-hour period. Despite being in pain and having difficulty walking. At the end of my shift, I immediately attended the Accident and Emergency Department at The Royal Preston Hospital. Fortunately, it was quiet and I didn't have to wait long to be assessed by the doctor. Thankfully, my foot wasn't fractured but sprained. I was being advised to rest it as much as possible. With Christmas only a few days away all of it seemed highly impossible.

"It's my fortieth birthday today and I'm going to die." I said to myself, as the sweat began to pour off my face and body. It was as though I'd just had a bath or shower. My tongue was beginning to stick to the roof of my mouth. "Are you all right Helen?" asked Sue. As the colour drained from my face and hands. I was trudging up a hill at the start of a walk. Chris was due to be married that Saturday afternoon. It was my fortieth birthday on the day of the walk, and Anne's birthday was on the following day. Friends and colleagues, known as "The rambling midwives," working on our maternity unit. Regularly walked at various countryside locations. They'd organised this hike through the Lancashire countryside to celebrate our three special occasions.

Making a beehive for a boulder of stone, which lay conveniently at the top of the hill. I plumped myself on it. Sue passed me water to drink, and tissues to wipe my drenched face. They all reassured me by saying, "this is the worst part of the trek. There aren't any more hills the rest of the way." As I arose, they noticed that I'd sat on cow dung, which was lying on top of the rock. The girls were right. It was much easier now. I was no longer puffing and blowing. Feeling as though I was at death's door.

It was the Lancashire countryside at its best. We were walking in Whitewell. A small village in the Ribble valley in the forest of Bowland. Following which we were due to have lunch at The Inn at Whitewell. A picturesque, sprawling, small rural inn/restaurant and hotel. As we stumbled over a wooden fence into another farmer's field, which was muddier than the previous one. My right boot had become stuck in the mud, as I hadn't tightened my shoelaces adequately. As I attempted to free myself, the wet, soft earth was splattered everywhere. Over my once clean blue tracksuit, which was now blue with splashes of brown.

By this time, the group was spread out. The keen walkers way out in front. The straggling left trailing behind. Laughing and talking as we wandered along. Eventually, after about three hours we saw the Inn at Whitewell in the distance, signalling the end of our saunter. There was already a table prepared for us. Resplendent against the rolling green, grassy, sleepy meadows. A colourful hue of flowers, trees, and plants swaying gently in the breezy sunshine.

My eyes were deceiving me. There were my parents standing on the stairway of Auntie Oddie's house. A look of delight on their faces, as the taxi taking me there from the airport had arrived. My ninety-seven-year-old grandmother was ill, and I was desperate to see her. Working extra nights to facilitate my ten-day trip. They were only in New York by default, as their flight to Trinidad that morning had been overbooked. They were leaving in two days' time making it the ideal opportunity for us to spend some time together. It was also wonderful to receive a visit from my high school friend Dianne who lived and worked as a dentist in the city. The terminal building at the airport was in lockdown at the time of my departure back to England. The trial of those suspected of the terrorist attempt of the World Trade Centre in 1993 was being held.

I was continuously feeling cold and exhausted, as though my body would come to a complete standstill. It was a struggle working three nights a week and tending to a family and home. I would arrive at Asda Supermarket saying to myself, "hold on to the trolley and walk along with it." Even at work I'd fall asleep standing upright for seconds at a time. It was pure will power, resolve and determination to keep myself moving. Following a visit to my doctor, I was diagnosed with an underactive thyroid gland, with an extremely low thyroid function test result. Requiring the treatment of Thyroxine to be taken every day for the rest of my life.

There was an extreme state of excitement in the Brathwaite household. It was the fifth of August 1996. The children and I were due to leave for New York/Chicago on the following morning. The first of its kind, The Mottley family reunion was being held on the long weekend commencing Thursday the 8th to Sunday the 11th of August 1996. Staying overnight at Auntie Oddie's home in Brooklyn. Then travelling onwards to Chicago.

Wonderful to see my grandmother again, I was anxious for the boys to become acquainted with her once more. Following our visit in 1988, and for Natalie to meet her for the first time. Collected by Lois and her two young sons, Brett, seven, and Rhys, five at the airport. She was intent on receiving her supplies of Mars Bars and Quality Street chocolates, which we'd brought for her from Preston. As soon as we'd gathered our luggage from the carousel.

Most of the family were already at Brian and Lois's home, and at various hotels in the area. The scene when we arrived there reminded me of the film "Home Alone," as Joe Pesci stood at the foot of the stairs. People everywhere, and family members ascending and descending the staircase. A very spacious home, with three reception rooms, huge kitchen and pantry, utility room, dining room, downstairs toilet, and bathroom, one bedroom, a massive basement overflowing with toys. With four further bedrooms upstairs with walk in wardrobes, a luxurious ensuite to the master bedroom, and a further family toilet and bathroom. At the back of the home was a large, wooden veranda, with barbecue equipment. Wooden steps leading to swings, and a slide alongside it. Beyond that lay a beautiful man-made lake.

Before I even awoke on the following morning, Edward, Erle, and Natalie were already up and dressed. Had had breakfast, and had disappeared into the basement, and outside on the swings and slide, with all their cousins. There were so many toys, games, and activities to share around, that there were no disagreements amongst them. They played so harmoniously together. The older children looking after the younger ones. The adults chattering and laughing. Reminiscing about years gone by. Busily we prepared for the late afternoon and evening's werlcome barbecue. It all began with a prayer of thanksgiving to commence the weekend's family celebrations by Brian and Lois's church minister, followed by a celebratory dinner on the following evening. Boarding the metro train from Aurora into Chicago on the Saturday morning for a sight-seeing tour of the windy city, proceeded by a boat trip on Lake Michigan. Arriving home at midnight. I've no idea how we made it to the 9A.M Sunday Morning service. A lunch time picnic at Lake Warbonsie, Aurora, brought the reunion to an end. One of my lasting memories of this time was a photograph taken of my grandmother, with her great grand-children standing beside her, as she sat amongst them.

"Are you awake, mum?" asked Natalie breathlessly. It was 12.45P.M on a Saturday afternoon. She'd just run up the stairs, two at a time. Attempting to prise open my eyes, as I lay in bed asleep after working the night before. She had a swimming lesson every Saturday at 2P.M. We arrived there all in a blur. My eyes glazed over from lack of sleep. Siobhan, another midwife, who worked with me on the previous night, sat ghost like on the little benches at the side of the pool, feeling and looking like zombies. Fighting hard to keep awake. Attempting to watch our daughters Helen and Natalie swim. I was relieved that Eddie was off duty that day and was at home preparing a meal for the family. Once I'd eaten I was free to return to bed. Able to enjoy a blissful sleep, before returning for another night shift that evening. Occasionally it wasn't that straight forward. Not if we both happened to be working. As I'd have to prepare a meal myself on return from swimming. Not having the appropriate opportunity to have adequate rest before returning to work that evening.

Lois, Brett, Rhys, and Patricia were arriving in London at 6.30 A.M from Paris. They were staying in the city overnight, then leaving for Dublin later the following day. Natalie, Erle, and I had travelled by the early morning train from Preston to see them. Together we enjoyed a wonderful day sightseeing, shopping, and having dinner together before we returned to Preston on the last evening train.

The post-natal ward was swarming with patients. The sound of screaming babies, and the vibration of patient call bells continued to reverberate in my ears. My two-week-old headache had worsened. By 5A.M that morning I could no longer concentrate on what I was doing. Asking Margaret, another midwife to check my blood pressure as I believed that it could have been elevated. A flicker of concern appeared and then as swiftly vanished from her face as she checked it. Asking Barbara to review her findings. "Is it all right?" I asked them. They both said," It is high. 180/120." Barbara contacted Veronica, senior midwifery sister working on Delivery Suite, who requested that I come down to see her. Greeting me at the entrance as I arrived there. Ushering me into one of the rooms. Making me comfortable, sat in an armchair. Offering me a cup of tea and toast. Wiring me up to the blood pressure machine, which took and registered my vital signs at regular intervals. "As soon as your doctor's surgery opens this morning. Make an urgent appointment, taking this with you. Don't return until you're feeling better," she said as she handed me the copy of my blood pressure recordings. At 11 A.M that morning, I handed Dr Smith the document, prompting him to check my blood pressure. Immediately prescribing me Atenolol 100mgs, a betablocker used to treat the illness, to be taken orally once a day. This made me feel very sleepy and drowsy. Signing me off work for eight weeks.

It was eight "O" clock on a bleak, windy, freezing, overcast, wintry Sunday morning. I'd just driven unto my driveway, as Edward was on his way to do his paper round. Coughing continuously. His eyes and nose red, with clear fluid dripping like a tap from them. It was in stark contrast from when I'd left him to go to work the evening before. As he approached me, he said with a croaky voice. "Mum, my throat feels sore, I'm feeling very tired as I've hardly slept, with coughing all night. I've got this paper round to do and I don't think I can do it." "I'll help you with it before I go to bed. It will be too late for the newsagent to get a replacement for you." Quickly we'd completed the round. Returning home to warm, welcoming beds.

Increasingly we'd become honorary taxi drivers. Transporting the children to all their varying activities Continuously working opposite each other to care for our offspring. Eddie would arrive home following an evening shift, leaving the engine running. We would then have a brief handover. Then I'd be rushing out of the front door, out to work.

Broughton Church Choir was singing both Sunday services at Liverpool Cathedral. The Church of England Cathedral of the diocese of Liverpool. I was working the night before, and we were all travelling there to support him. Due to time owing, I was leaving work at 03.30A.M. Having about four hours sleep, before setting off for Liverpool. By the time the evening devotional had come along, tiredness had finally caught up with me. I was finding it impossible to keep my eyes opened and began to snore loudly. Eddie and Erle, seated either side of me, began to nudge me.

Unable to sleep, I glanced at the clock on the bedside table. It was only 1.30 A.M. For the past two hours I'd been tossing and turning in bed. Eddie wasn't able to sleep either. "What's the matter? Why haven't you been able to settle?" He asked me. "I don't know. I have a strange feeling that something's happened to my grandmother." I replied. Eventually snatching five minutes of sleep. I was awoken by the telephone's shrilly ringing from the hallway downstairs just five minutes later. I managed to get to the phone before it stopped ringing. It was my sister Pat, calling me from Trinidad. My grandmother had just died. Carmelita Davina Mottley was born in February 1898.She was one-hundred-and-two. The alluring aroma of freshly baked bread filled the house as I opened my front door after seeing Natalie off for school. My grandmother always made her own bread. I suspected that she'd come to wish me goodbye.

By the end of my night shift, I'd become known as the "computer whiz kid," The usage of technology had become more widespread within the N.H.S. I was forty-five years old and had never used the electronic device! The cursor appeared to be out of control, as it darted wildly across the screen. "I thought you said that had a computer at home!" Exclaimed Jeanette, who was supervising me. "I do, but I've never used it."

Carolynn, Maggie, and I had rushed unto the train, as the automatic doors were about to close. We collapsed breathlessly on our seats on our way to Salford University for a study day. We were now required to fulfil about ten of these, instead of the week-long residential courses. Arriving there about an hour later. Registering for the day. Meeting other midwives from hospitals throughout the Northwest of England.

Trying as much as I could, I couldn't manage to pull my uniform over my head. I was standing in front of my locker, in the staff changing room. It took time and patience, and help from my colleagues, to dress myself satisfactorily for work. Over the past week, the intensity of the pain in my right shoulder had increased, with diminishing movement. Arriving at my doctor's surgery two hours after finishing work. Seen and examined by Dr Parker with the diagnosis of a frozen shoulder. Administering a Hydrocortisone injection in the bone of my right shoulder. Referring me to Jill. The physiotherapist who worked at the practise.

My parent's fiftieth wedding anniversary was due soon. The date due to fall on the 24th of March 2001. Financially planning our journey in advance, by way of the Air Mile Scheme. Mostly shopping at Sainsbury's Supermarket. One hundred points being allocated to each packet of bacon, of which I bought countless amounts. Also using the awards given to each grocery shop. This enabled us to obtain two free air tickets. Arriving in Trinidad and Tobago in July 2001 for our second family reunion celebrating our parents' golden nuptials. It involved visiting beaches, the pitch lake, and Asa Wright Nature Resort, meals, and barbecues. Returning to England at the middle of August.

Mobility problems with my frozen shoulder limited me to working only on the ante/ post-natal wards. Amongst one of my patients one evening was Julie Smith. A mother of two boys from her first marriage. This was her third pregnancy by her second husband, and her labour was to be induced on the following morning on Delivery Suite as her due date of delivery had already passed by ten days. She intended to have a warm, relaxing bath before going to bed, to calm her anxieties about the next morning's events.

About five minutes later, the patient call bell was set off by Julie. Her contractions had suddenly started, and the birth was imminent. I rushed to her aid. Quickly getting her out of the bath. Ringing the alarm bell for assistance as I did so. Drying her skin swiftly, helping her to put on her nightdress. Not even thinking about the problems with my shoulder. Rushing towards her bed, getting there just in time, as she gave birth to a beautiful baby girl. Suddenly, there was an eruption of cheering women who'd gathered, around the four bedded bay.

Mike, Julie's husband rushed unto the ward about twenty-five minutes later, looking as though he'd climbed through a hedge backwards, as the midwives had awoken him from a restful sleep. Letting him know of his daughter's arrival. He also looked like a child who'd received no presents on Christmas morning. This all changed as soon as he saw his female infant. His eyes lit up like a Christmas tree. You couldn't wipe the smile off his face. He held her so close to him that you would have thought someone was attempting to snatch her away from him. Julie herself was grinning from ear to ear, and her eyes shone with happiness.

Worsened by the extra strain put on my shoulder, my physiotherapy sessions for my frozen shoulder treatment increased. I then heard the news that my mother had become seriously ill. Her stomach had been bleeding due to the side effects of her medication. I decided to visit her as soon as I could, preferring to see her whilst she was alive, and to spend quality time with her. It was March 2002. I'd already had a week's holiday booked and another week's compassionate leave. My sister Lois was also on holiday. Both arriving in Trinidad at the same time.

My mother looked surprisingly well with her eyes lighting up as soon as she saw us. My father, on the other hand was the colour of an orange. His clothing dropping off his body. I knew then that his time on earth was rapidly diminishing. He'd been diagnosed with prostate cancer by his doctor five years previously. It was a blessing that Lois and I were currently at home to enable us to have this precious two weeks with our parents.

Chapter Thirteen

There was a sudden loud noise which startled me, coming from the left sided front passenger side of our car, where I was seated. My head shifted to the right, and then just as rapidly, fully rebounded on itself like that of a ragdoll. My left occiput clashing into the post between the two doors. In that split second, I began to feel sick with the pain. Almost experiencing a state of collapse. Feeling cold and clammy, with my hands beginning to shake like the leaves on a tree on a windy day.

I instinctively began rubbing the left side of my head. Hearing explosions within it, like bonfire night. The fireworks continuously detonating, as tears trickled down my cheeks. Eddie, who was driving the vehicle, brought it to a standstill. "Are you ok?" He asked me. "Yes." I replied. An elderly silver haired man, wearing a grey Andy Capp flat cap, and a matching jacket, had also pulled up in front of us. He had appeared at the damaged side of our automobile. First examining the smashed doors. Eddie joined him, whereupon they exchanged all the relevant document details.

It was just after midday on Wednesday the 21st of August 2002. We were on our way to Preston train station, to purchase tickets for our twelve-year-old daughter, Natalie, and me, for a day trip to Edinburgh, early the following morning. Travelling there via Moor Lane and The Adelphi Roundabout, where the collision occurred. The other motorcar having entered the busy junction via Walker Street, immediately following Moor Lane. Fortunately, there was no need to contact the police, as there was already a police officer in the vicinity. Providing assistance and advice. Giving us a piece of rope to tie together our bashed in left front door, with the left back door, as they hadn't been able to close. Such was the impact of the crash. We then managed to make our way at a snail's pace to the station.

This was a bustling hub, one of many, on the West coast main line. Halfway between London and Scotland. Full of holiday revellers, and a long queue at the ticket office. It took hours for us to be served. I felt as though I was being tortured as my left occiput continued to throb uncontrollably. It took self-control for me not to break down in tears. I fought extremely hard to conquer the thoughts of immediately returning home, without buying the tickets. Instead persevering by steadfastly remaining in the line of waiting people.

It took another lifetime for us to get home. A journey that normally took twenty minutes, taking over an hour. By the time we did manage to get there, I was snapping at everyone. I couldn't get anything done. "Why don't you go to A and E?" Eddie suggested. I didn't need to be asked twice. Arriving there within ten minutes. The hospital being a short walk away from our home. It was terribly busy as I'd arrived. Seen in the first instance by a triage nurse, followed by an extended period of waiting before being reviewed by a doctor. A diagnosis of bruising and soft tissue injury to the left side of my head, neck, and shoulder was made. I was advised to take some pain killers, and to make a follow up appointment with my G.P, Dr Smith.

I didn't feel fit enough to travel by train early the following morning. This was a girl's day out which Natalie and I had been planning for weeks. I didn't want to disappoint her. Armed with sufficient pain killers, we made our way to Edinburgh, making the most of the dawning beautiful day. Up at five "O'clock that morning, in readiness for getting the early train there. It was brand new, with about eight carriages.

I almost died climbing the slope leading up to the castle, situated at the top of The Royal Mile. Seating arrangements all prepared for the Tattoo. An annual musical event by international performers, with pomp, majesty, and ceremony. Viewing the honours of Scotland, the crown, sceptre, and the sword of state. Boarding all four tour buses to include all arears of the city. Getting the last train returning to Preston.

It wasn't until the following morning that my entire body felt stiff and painful, following the walk up the hill to the castle, and around the hilly streets of the municipality. My head, neck, shoulders, and left arm continued to be sore. I continually took analgesia to control the pain. There were remnants of aching, which had continued from my frozen shoulder injury

I Will Survive

of the previous year. I'd struggled to work with discomfort, exhaustion, and headaches. Having about twelve months of physiotherapy treatments.

My week's holiday was ending. Coping with the increasing twinges was becoming difficult to manage. I began to pace myself during the day. Finding listening to music, and singing therapeutic, and relaxing. I tried to be as positive as I could. As this attracts more positivity. Having faith in God, and myself, that my condition would eventually improve. I was dreading returning to work, but reluctant to cause any staff shortages in our unit. I was fearful of letting my colleagues down. I managed to work a total of four nights, but it was a battle to perform my duties as a midwife. All the awkward positions that we find ourselves working in. I found it difficult to concentrate. My job was a very responsible one. I was accountable for the care of mother and baby. Including the administration of controlled medication, used antenatally, during labour, and postnatally. I found myself taking stronger pain relief medication to control the pain.

Things came to a head one night. I was feeding a baby. I must have fallen asleep for just a second. I awoke to find that while continuing to firmly hold the infant. My arms were almost touching the floor. Horrified, I knew that I couldn't continue to place lives at risk. Not telling anyone about the incident. I informed the senior midwife of the unit, that I felt unwell, and was unable to continue my shift.

Chapter Fourteen

I had an appointment with Dr Smith, which I'd arranged that morning. He had been our family doctor since 1983. A very pleasant man, about forty-eight years old. With blonde bushy hair and moustache. I explained to him what had happened at the time of my accident and what had occurred since then. He asked me if he could examine my neck. The thought of him doing this made me feel all the muscles in my body tighten and recoil. Especially those of my neck and shoulders, anticipating the pain that it would cause.

I was required to move my neck through a range of movements. Rotating and tilting my head from one side, to the other. Then bending and extending it. These proved to be limited. I was referred to Jill, the physiotherapist who treated me for my frozen shoulder, until a few months ago. He'd also signed me off work for a period of two weeks. Prescribing Co-Proxamol, an analgesic to treat moderate pain, and Diclofenac 25 mgs, helping to reduce inflammation and pain, by preventing the production of chemicals, which cause swelling, pain, and stiffness. Improving movement in the affected area. He also requested a neck Xray to confirm whether there was any damage to the neck.

Advised to take two Co-Proxamol every four hours. I realised that on doing this I'd sleep all day. Finding it better to take one tablet on each occasion, in between Diclofenac every four hours. This made me sleepy but still drowsy. Especially at night, when I took Atenolol 100 mgs for the treatment of high blood pressure. I was beginning to feel permanently drunk. Towards the end of September 2002, the pain began to travel down my left arm. A weird tingly sensation. Two weeks later, a similar feeling on the left side of my face commenced. The gums of the left side of my mouth would also pulsate, and with each throb, the pain would intensify.

Jill had continued my treatments in early October. She had been qualified as a physiotherapist for twenty-five years and seemed understanding of my difficulties. She knew exactly what I was talking about, when I described to her what had happened to me, and the symptoms I was experiencing. Using treatments such as therapeutic ultrasound. This is a method of encouraging the healing of damaged tissue, underneath the skin. Using high frequency sound waves by using a transducer and gel. Resulting in increased blood flow to the area, speeding up the healing process.

Jill performed various neck exercises to encourage movement. Turning my head from one side to the other. Bending my neck to one side, and then the other. Bending my head fully, then completely extending it. She instructed me to do these exercises daily at home, and at appointments with her. Before each treatment began, the effectiveness of the exercises and treatment was judged at how well I performed them. I also used heat therapy at home with an electric heating pad, to provide pain relief, relieve muscle spasm and promote healing. Jill was about forty-three years old. Of petite build. Attractive, with a rounded face, and a pixie like haircut. We would talk about our children, and sporting events, such as cricket, football, and athletics. Bantering about English/ West Indies cricket.

I focused all my energy on getting through my days the best I could. This included having regular breaks between conducting my household chores. Taking much longer to complete than they normally would. Finding listening and singing along to music whilst I did them fulfilling. Helping me to cope with the pain, by feeling happy and relaxed. Caused by the natural release of endorphins. The brain's feel good chemicals. Releasing more oxygen into the bloodstream, encouraging better circulation. Promoting cheerfulness and reducing anxiety. Having a deep faith in God. That I would be guided by him through these challenging times. Helping me to become an even stronger person, able to cope with any problems.

Jill was stunned one morning. I'd rung her from the bus station. "Where are you?" She asked me. "You're supposed to be here." "You won't believe where I am. I don't know what happened, but I forgot all about my appointment. Didn't get off the bus, ending up at the bus station." I informed her. "Come straight here. Don't worry about it. I'll also rebook you to see Dr Smith, as you've also missed that consultation." She replied. I boarded the same bus that brought me to the bus terminal. Following this, the driver would always make a point of asking me whether I intended to get off at that stop.

Our car was written off. An accident insurance claim had begun. My neck X ray was normal. Eddie and I were also allocated different solicitors as the responsibility for the cause of the accident, was being disputed. There would also have been a possibility of a conflict of interest. In December 2002, my extensive course of physiotherapy was completed. I was assessed by Dr France, a G.P with regards to my accident claim. He made light of my description of my symptoms. The weird, tingly feeling going down my left arm and hand originating from my neck. Finding it difficult to believe that anyone would experience such side effects from their medication. He recommended that I be reviewed by a neurologist or neurosurgeon. To ascertain the cause of my symptoms, to which he was unsure were caused by the collision. He queried whether there was any additional pathology accountable for my neurological manifestations, and neck discomfort. He couldn't justify why I would work when I was in so much discomfort. He didn't understand my work ethic. I'd gone to work with extreme tiredness before being diagnosed with an under active thyroid. Hardly able to walk with a badly bruised foot. Working with a persistent headache for two weeks before being identified as having high blood pressure. Unable to move my frozen shoulder. I'd have to be dead not to be at my place of employment. I didn't agree with his report to settle my claim. I continued to have regular sessions with Dr Smith. Continuing to supply me with sick notes as I was incapable of working. Being referred to and placed on a waiting list for review by a consultant neurologist.

On the 27th of January 2003. I received the sad news that my father had passed away. It was the day of his 79th birthday. Natalie and I began arrangements to attend his funeral. His burial service appeared to be attended by the entire population of Trinidad and Tobago. My siblings, myself, and other family members were there to support my mother. Even though she was crippled by rheumatoid arthritis. She stood tall and dignified. Thankfully on return to England on the 15th of February 2003. The snow and ice in abundance when we were leaving, had completely disappeared.

Chapter Fifteen

The physiotherapy treatments during the months of October to December 2002 had successfully pushed my neck and shoulder pain on the back burner. With the advancing wintry weather, my left facial and head discomfort progressed. My cheek felt as though it had been touched gently with a piece of cotton wool, or at worst slapped with a hand. The gums would throb continuously, and each time become more painful. As the hurting increased, I began taking two Co-Proxamol together, alternating with Tramadol. This increased my feelings of drunkenness. As the howling wind travelled up my legs, back, and neck, through my clothing. My fingers and hands would become cold, numb, sore and red. Tears would flow uncontrollably down my left cheek. My feet would feel like tree trunks, frozen and difficult to move.

The agony would then travel downwards from the left side of my neck, through my shoulder, arm, and hand. With electrical impulses filtering down and out through my fingers. A similar effect could be felt also from the left side of my neck, and upwards into the left side of my head and face. I was forced to add items of clothing to my wardrobe, that I wouldn`t have been caught dead in previously. Thermals, tights, socks, jumpers, three-layer jackets, hats, gloves, about seven scarves, and a balaclava.

I was in Preston City Centre, within the vicinity of St Georges Shopping Centre. My entire body began to shake like a leaf as it was very cold, rainy, and windy. There were groups of researchers gathered around. Encouraging passers-by to complete surveys on everyday shopping items via computers, from one of the vacant buildings nearby. As one of them approached me, she said, "Come in here with me, (pointing to the nearby building) have a cup of tea and a biscuit, sit by the fire, keep warm, while you do some surveys."

My six months full pay on sick leave had just been completed. I was now in receipt of half of my normal wages. I was stood in line at my bank, edging closer and closer to the top of the queue. Slightly embarrassed and not wishing anyone to hear my enquiries. I almost whispered. "Can you give me the balances of my savings accounts please." The grand total came to the regal sum of £3.00. I was desperate. I needed to do food shopping. As she handed me my money, I asked her, "Is it possible to speak to a personal banker please?" Guided to a private room to await the arrival of Jessica, an elegantly dressed young woman of about twenty-five. "How can I help you, Mrs Brathwaite?" She asked me. "Can you possibly lend me five pounds until Tuesday, when I get my Incapacity Benefit payment?" "Have you not got anyone who can lend you some money? The bank isn't a charity." She informed me. Just as she'd finished the sentence I began to cry. "Please help me!" I pleaded. At this point, she called the bank manager, who signed a form granting me permission to receive £5.00 from the cashier. Desperate for financial help, I visited the tax office for advice. Child tax credits had recently been introduced by the government. Our family had had about three payments, but at the rate which suited our monetary arrangements when we were both employed. As I informed my advisor of our predicament, she asked me," how are you managing? I'll sort something out for you by tomorrow morning." She reassured me. I shed tears of joy as I stood at the A.T.M machine on the following day. There was the money in my account as she had promised. It was wonderful to do a proper food shop again. To make things stretch I was using one tea bag three or four times. Adding water to the milk till it looked anaemic and making my own bread.

Harry Potter and the Chamber of Secrets was being shown at The Odeon Cinema. Natalie And I couldn't afford to go. However, if she collected Dairy Lea Lunchable vouchers. She would have been offered free tickets in exchange by the cinema. In April 2003 I had an appointment with Dr Sparrow, consultant neurologist. Explaining to him what occurred at the accident and the problems I'd experienced since then. I was prescribed Amitriptyline 25mgs, to be taken at night, and a CT head scan was ordered by him. On taking the tablet that night, I immediately became very drowsy. It was as though I was floating in mid-air. I couldn't feel myself walking on the flooring at home. Neither on the pavements, or on the streets outside my home. I was permanently drowsy twenty-four hours a day. I'd forgotten

I Will Survive

how to cross the road safely and would wander across the streets without safety checks. Receiving in reply, angry tooting of horns, and sometimes abusive language from drivers.

I became the sleeping cook. I'd wake up to find that the wooden spoon had disappeared to the bottom of the pan. I'd mix up all the cooking ingredients. Sometimes my family would refuse to eat whatever I'd prepared. I also forgot to turn off the gas oven, and cooker on numerous occasions. Putting myself, my family, and neighbours at risk.

One morning, I was on my way downstairs with my washing basket in hand. I lost my footing, falling down the stairs. My glasses had become dislodged from my face, landing on the last step, where upon I'd sat on them. They'd become bent and twisted. There was also a trail of soiled clothing all the way down the staircase. The basket had finally found it's resting place in the middle of the hallway, whilst the lid lay in splendour half-way down the flight of stairs. Gathering all my laundry, I placed them in my washing machine. Deciding to make bread, I put two loaves snuggled in their baking tins in the grill, which was situated directly above the oven set on a low temperature, to enable the bread to rise. Then entering my back garden to hang my washing on the line. I could only remember lifting my clothing in my arms. I had no recollection of what happened next. There was my washing strewn all over the lawn. At that moment, I could smell something burning. I ran into the kitchen, finding that there were two loaves of half-baked and burnt bread. Surprised to find that I'd also ignited the grill. I didn't know whether to laugh or cry! Somehow, I managed to do both! I needed to redo the washing, and a new batch of dough. The receptionist at my optician's looked puzzled as she examined my glasses. "How on earth did you manage to do that?" She asked. I sweetly smiled at her, offering no reply. I was convinced that she wouldn't have believed me, if I'd confided in her what had happened.

I would have made an excellent guest at a Greek wedding. I continually broke glasses, plates, cups, dishes, pans, pressure cookers. I just couldn't feel myself holding them. So, they would always end up smashed, twisted, and broken on the floor. My symptoms weren't improving by the time of my second appointment with Dr Sparrow. He increased the dosage to 50 mgs at night. He diagnosed me with a typical facial pain. Things only worsened! I caused havoc wherever I went. At my bank branch, there was always someone waiting at the door, especially to deal with me, as I'd dropped half of my bills and money on the floor, without realising it. Denying that they were mine, until I got to the cashier and noticed that they were missing. As I attempted to place a plastic bottle of tomato ketchup which I'd gotten from the supermarket shelf into my trolly, it broke away from my grasp, falling to the ground. Skating down the aisle, with a trail of its red sauce following closely behind it.

"I don't know where I'm going!" I declared to the bus driver as I boarded the No 19 bus from the bus station. "It's all right. I know where you're going." He reassured me. Dropping me off at the top of my street. Almost walking out of a supermarket without paying, prompted me to make an appointment with my G.P, to discuss with him all my concerns about the problems I was experiencing with my medication. He stopped the Amitriptyline, requesting an urgent review with Dr Sparrow, and prescribing Nortriptyline 10 mgs instead.

From feeling like a zombie, walking on air twenty-four hours a day. It was wonderful to be once more aware of myself walking on terra firma. The pain which was lessened by Amitriptyline was at its fore once more. Physiotherapy treatments had recommenced with Jill. My neck pain had never stopped. Jill suggested using acupuncture as a method of pain relief. Recollecting my childhood in Trinidad, my grandmother would prepare herbal treatments which she used on herself. As quickly as my mind wandered back to the past, it returned to the present. Then I thought to myself, "well, why not?"

We chatted as she inserted the fine acupuncture needles in parts of the left side of my head, neck, shoulder, and down my arm and hand. I felt a feeling of calm, relaxation, serenity, and well-being spread around my body. I felt tired and sleepy, and immediately nodded off to sleep. The effects of the treatment took the edge off my pain. It didn't incapacitate me as it was short acting. I began having it regularly, as, and when I required it, in addition to taking my other analgesia daily as required. My greatest wish was to have acupuncture daily, but that would have been impossible.

"Help me Natalie Wan Kenobi. You're my only hope." I announced to her as she came in from school, expecting me to be dressed, ready for an acupuncture session. Followed by a shopping trip to Asda. I was unable to get my top on and was waiting for her to help me with that. Eddie and

Natalie assisted me with doing the household chores, but there were times when it wasn't available. To enable me to hang the washing on the line. I used a clothing basket on wheels, which I would place under the item I was about to fasten with clothes pegs. I would also sing along and dance to my music, at maximum volume to keep me awake, and to assist me in focusing on whatever I was doing, whether it was cooking, vacuuming, or washing dishes.

Even though Nortriptyline was milder than Amitriptyline. The side effects continued to be troublesome. I'd received my medical report from Dr Spinner. Consultant neurologist, with regards to my accident claim. I disagreed fully with his report. I was disappointed that he couldn't understand that I was sensitive to the effects of my medication, and that I hadn't returned to work as a midwife. It was essential that I had to be 100% fit. A midwife works under sometimes stressful life or death situations. Responsible for accurate record keeping, and reporting. I wasn't capable of carrying out these responsibilities. I refused to put my life or others at risk.

As a review meeting with Dr Sparrow and his team. Nortriptyline was discontinued, and I was discharged from his care, as there wasn't anything else that they could do for me. At times, I found it difficult not to feel sorry for myself. Especially during the cold, winter months, when my body became extremely sensitive to the effects of the cold, wind, and rain. I found myself adding more clothing to my wardrobe. I came to be known as "Captain Scott of the Antarctic," as I wandered around Preston, wearing socks, thermals, jumpers, three-layer jackets, thick woollen fleecy trousers, scarves, hats, and a balaclava. I also bought Micky and Minnie Mouse shopping bags. Calling them my cheer me up bags when going out. Tears would trickle down my left cheek, which would become red and swollen. Sometimes my lips would become inflamed too. I would then shiver uncontrollably.

One breezy, cold, winter's morning. I was standing at the kitchen sink, doing the washing up and looking out through the window. I felt my mood sinking, becoming sad and miserable. When the voice of Louis Armstrong began filling my kitchen via the radio, with the words, "I see trees of green, red roses too. I see them bloom for me and you, and I think to myself what a wonderful world. I see skies so blue and clouds so white. The bright blessed day, the dark sacred night, and I think to myself what a wonderful world.

The colours of the rainbow so pretty in the sky are also on the faces of people going by. I see friends shaking hands saying how do you do. They're really saying I love you. I hear babies' cry; I watch them grow. They'll learn much more than I'll ever know. And I think to myself what a wonderful world. Yes, I think to myself what a wonderful world. Yes, I think to myself what a wonderful world." My tears began to flow. I realised that I had so much to be grateful for. I was alive. I could see. I could hear. I could walk. I could speak. I could sing and dance.

Edward's friend had been seriously injured in a road traffic accident. His life was all but non-existent. I was in pain but I wasn't dead. At that moment, I recalled being in the school choir, as a fourteen-year-old, singing "count your blessings one by one," and "Oh music sweet."

"Count your blessings one by one when dawn appears, and day has just begun. They will light your heart with happiness. Make each hour bright and bring your gladness. Count your blessings one by one, when twilight falls, and toil of day is done. And in sweet dreams they'll come again to you. If you will count your blessings each day through. Count your blessings while you may, for we are here but little time to stay. All around are hearts sincere and true. Lovely things abound just waiting for you. Count your blessings while you may. The big or small, whichever comes your way. For then you'll find this world a place of love. If you will count your blessings from above."

"Oh, Music Sweet." Oh, music sweet in many precious moments. When sorrow falls and skies are grey above. Within my heart a loving fire is kindled. My soul awakes in a world of joy and love. My soul awakes in joy and love. How oft a sigh has gently set in motion. Upon my harp a chord of memories enshrine. Upon my soul a heavenly peace descending. Oh, music sweet that in my heart doth reign. Oh, music sweet my life is thine." At that tender age, I never understood the true meaning of those words. It was then that I knew how much music meant to me. How important it is to anyone's soul, body, spirit, and mind. It uplifts you. Making you happy. I took every opportunity I could to go out, as it can be so beneficial to anyone's wellbeing. Just to be out in the fresh air. Seeing other people and being a part of the local community. My mother had been crippled by rheumatoid arthritis for years. I always remember her saying to me." I'll always be in pain. Whether I stay at home or go out. So, I dress smartly, venture out and enjoy myself." She had a great philosophy. Many times, she, and Mrs Awon, our next-door neighbour, would dress elegantly and go to the Hilton for afternoon tea.

On the 5th of February 2004. A meeting was convened between myself, and my employers, to discuss my future. I indicated to them that my health hadn't improved. That I continued to experience a considerable amount of pain. Especially during the autumn/winter months. It was unlikely that I would be fit to return to work in any capacity, soon. Therefore, the option of redeployment wasn't appropriate. As a result, my contract was terminated with immediate effect. On the grounds of capability. My managers were deeply sorry to lose my service of more than twenty-one years. Thanking me for all my efforts in the past. I was paid the maximum notice period of twelve weeks in lieu of a tax-free lump sum. In my final salary, I also received a sum of money equivalent to thirty working days, in lieu of outstanding annual leave.

Chapter Sixteen

Following my discharge from the neurologist, and a referral to the pain clinic. I attended my first appointment at the department. Dr Onions, consultant anaesthetist introduced himself to me. We discussed my medical history, and my required treatment. Enquiring of me whether I was willing to participate in the programme. Advising me to discuss the events with my husband Eddie. Returning later for the procedure, called a Stellate Ganglion Block.

A stellate ganglion block is an injection of local anaesthetic in the sympathetic nerve tissue, in the neck. Its purpose is to block the sympathetic nerves that supply the arms and face. This may hopefully reduce pain and swelling. Helping to increase mobility. Accompanied by Eddie., we were escorted by the nurse into the consulting treatment room at the day unit of our local hospital, who made me as comfortable as she could on the treatment bed. Wired up to vital signs machinery. Monitoring my blood pressure, pulse, and oxygen saturation. Dr Onions then gave me a small injection to numb the area, prior to the procedure taking place.

Even with this shot, the block was a very painful process to the back of my throat. I made the utmost effort to remain perfectly still and lifeless. I knew that should I wriggle or complain. It would take even longer. It was extremely unpleasant. With my neck feeling unbearably sore. Tears quickly gathered in my eyes and began to trickle down my cheeks. I immediately became floppy, and drowsy. Feeling intoxicated and in a state of collapse. As the medical team scurried around frantically checking all my vital signs of pulse, blood pressure with quizzical looks of wonder on their faces. To reassure them, I mumbled "don't worry. I'm fine. I'm sensitive to alcohol and prescribed medication." Dr Onions was finding it difficult to believe

I Will Survive

what was happening. He repeatedly said. "I've never had this problem before. All my patients usually recover quickly."

Transferred to the recovery ward, I remained under observation for four hours. I continued to be floppy, drowsy, and asleep. Finally opening my eyes and awakening. The nurse offered me a cup of tea and biscuits before the medical staff discharged me. On arrival there, my neck continued to ache, with the pain increasing in intensity. In tears I rang Jill pleading for acupuncture. She advised me that should I have it, the Stellate Ganglion Block might not be as effective. Suggesting that I have the treatment later in the week. It was Monday afternoon. It was such a struggle. The agony becoming more uncomfortable. I was swallowing analgesia like smarties. By the Thursday night to the early hours of Friday morning, the tears flew thick and fast. I was up all night and unable to sleep. Watching reruns of "Only Fools and Horses." At 08.30 hours, I phoned my doctor's surgery to make an appointment for that morning.

Listening intently to my concerns was Dr Roberts who wrote a letter to Dr Onions regarding what had occurred. Requesting an urgent review. Also sending an email to Jill, asking her to contact me as soon as possible, so that I could make an acupuncture appointment with her. Booked in for that afternoon, she couldn't insert the needles fast enough. The relief was instantaneous. Relaxing my body at once. This was to be her last week working at the surgery. She was about to begin employment at the pain clinic.

Dr Onions was rising quickly from his seat, eagerly extending his hand to shake ours. That enquiring look had disappeared from his face. He positioned himself in a chair close to where we were seated. Losing no time in asking how I was. Discussing the problems of the previous visit. He explained that he was going to inject seven millilitres of Bupivacaine, instead of the ten millilitres normal dosage. Judging from what had occurred previously, he thought that it would aid my recovery, as less anaesthetic would be administered. As he began preparing for the procedure. I very quickly and quietly whispered to Eddie. "I'm sure Jill's had a word with him." The tears freely trickled down my cheeks as I lay as still as I could, once again. Immediately becoming very floppy and sleepy, but not as much as on the previous occasion. Coming to in the recovery ward was a matter of three hours. Shorter than my first treatment, with my neck not being as sore. Surprisingly, Dr Onions visited me whilst I was there. Shaking his head in disbelief.

Dr Smith had referred me to Mark Rogers. Another physiotherapist. On the day of my first appointment, it was cold, windy, and rainy. My face red and my hands sore and stiff. My eyes puffy from crying. I was in agony! I was dressed as though I'd just arrived from the North Pole. In so much pain that I couldn't stop weeping, as I began stripping off all my excess clothing. My hat, balaclava, seven scarves, three-layer jacket, cardigan, and a jumper. Placing them in my hat, scarf, and glove bag. Mark's eyes became as huge as flying saucers, as I'd removed my garments, item by item. The tearfulness increased as he examined my neck movements. I found it even more distressing, as it was a while since I'd had any acupuncture. He wasn't impressed with my grumpy behaviour. Expressing his feelings accordingly. "We're not going to get on, are we?" In reply, I said, "I'm not usually like this, but I'm in so much pain. Once I have acupuncture, I'll be fine." Reluctantly, he replied. "I don't do acupuncture, but if you're in agreement, I'll do your physio, and John can do your acupuncture." He gave me exercises to practice at home, with further appointments made for himself and John.

Dr Onions, deep in thought, was studying my blood results. He enquired about my alcohol consumption as my liver function tests were elevated. I informed him that I never drank. "It's probably my medication I've been taking." I informed him. He answered, "you haven't been taking enough of them to have such an effect on your liver." He completed another blood form, so that I could have the tests repeated before my next appointment. The time had come for my third Stellate Ganglion Block. He explained that he was only administering five millilitres of Bupivacaine, half the normal dosage. Once again, I immediately became floppy, and sleepy, but not as much as before. My time on the recovery ward was reduced by fifty percent. My liver function tests were again elevated.

I'd discussed my Income Protection Plan Policy with him, as my first application to the insurance company hadn't been approved. He kindly agreed to support me with my appeal. I posted the relevant documents by special delivery to them but had heard nothing. Having checked online, whether they'd been delivered to them and signed for. I noticed that they had been. I immediately telephoned them, expressing my concerns. They were insistent that my paperwork hadn't been received. Eddie and

I visited them at their head office in London. Their managing director apologised and reassured me that they'd received my application. I personally handed over a copy of the letter written by Dr Onions in support of my application, even though I'd posted one with it. A week later my appeal was successful.

After a period of four months, physiotherapy/acupuncture treatments by Mark and John were successfully completed. However, I continued to have regular acupuncture sessions by Jill, who was practising privately from her home. Eddie and I travelled by train to attend an appointment with Dr Roper, consultant psychiatrist, in connection with my accident insurance claim, within the vicinity of the Harley Street of Liverpool. He was a pleasant man, of short stature, chubby red cheeks, and of middle-age appearance.

He gave me a few questionnaires to complete, followed by a consultation with him. He believed I had an adjustment disorder. Someone who has great difficulty coping with or adjusting to stress in which they may have the inability to function. Experiencing anxiety, low self-esteem, sadness, depression, problems sleeping, and social isolation. He recommended that I would benefit from cognitive behaviour therapy and eye movement desensitisation. To manage problems positively with a positive mindset. Using coping mechanisms to deal with your problems.

I didn't agree with his diagnosis as there were problems with my neck caused by my accident which occurred on the 21st of August 2002, the root of all my symptoms, and that I was coping well under the circumstances. Always remaining positive even in the most negative of situations. Not being a victim but choosing to be a victor instead. I've always had a good sense of humour and was forever laughing and smiling. I met up with friends and colleagues from work. Using means and processes such as music, singing and dancing as an aid to performing household tasks and to maintain a well-balanced mental state.

Jill had given me the address and telephone number of a physiotherapist called Martha, who had opened a practise in Preston. By the time I'd made an appointment with her, it had been a while since I'd had any acupuncture. She was very pleasant, tall, and slim, with blonde hair tied back with a scrunchie. She welcomed me very warmly into her treatment room, making me comfortable. Taking my complete medical history. Examining my neck for range of movement and flexibility. Massaging it, my shoulders, back, arms with aromatherapy oils, which was very soothing, relaxing, and felt wonderful. She then inserted the fine acupuncture needles, one by one, into my left neck, shoulder, arm, hand, and left occiput. Leaving them in situ for about twenty minutes. Then carefully removing them. The pain relief was instantaneous, and so very calming. I dreamily awoke. Slowly rising from the treatment bed. As I sat in the reception room. She offered me a cup of tea and chocolate biscuits. She was insistent that she took me home, as I had remained sleepy.

After a year, the privilege of having my Income Protection Plan was reviewed by the insurance company. Two nurses visited me at home to perform an assessment of my health. Whether I could bend, pick up certain objects, walking. After reviewing a report from Dr Onions. They adjudged that I was fit to return to work. My payments were discontinued. Dr Onions discussed with me that he couldn't continue conducting my treatments. He further encouraged me to return to work. He wasn't convinced that there were sufficient signs of any underlying neurological problems. He advised me that I had to learn to live with the pain and concentrate on returning to work. He then discharged me from the pain clinic. I'd discussed his suggestion with my midwifery manager. She insisted that there was no way that I'd pass a return to work medical, and that I wasn't one hundred percent fit to perform my duties as a midwife.

I continued to receive acupuncture sessions from Martha about once a month, or as required. Her business encompassed several natural remedial treatments, such as homeopathy, aromatherapy, massages, Pilates, amongst others administered by the relevant professional. I was keen to try the services of Catherine, the homeopath. She was a very pleasant young woman, in her late twenties. We sat sipping tea and chatting over an hour-long consultation regarding my medical history. Speaking at length about my accident, and the aspects of my difficulties since. She prescribed Hypericum in potency 30C. Hypericum is a natural remedy for nerve injuries and pain or numbness. Pain which radiates or shoots from the point of injury, and is throbbing, hot, or a pinched nerve sensation. As with the Amitriptyline, and Stellate Ganglion Blocks, there was an improvement in the numbness of my little finger and the one next to it. How long could I continue with this? There seemed to be no end to the pain. Acupuncture, aromatherapy, massages, and homeopathy, as well as analgesia would help. However, there was no lasting relief. Following a discussion with Dr Smith, a request for a second opinion from another neurologist was made.

Fraught with uneasiness and anxiety, I'd banished myself into my kitchen. Nervously cleaning, and tidying cupboards, to avoid watching Trinidad and Tobago's Soca Warriors first encounter with Sweden. What a relief it was when the match concluded with a nil nil draw! It was the football world cup in Germany. The single goal headed by Dennis Lawrence had fired The Soca Warriors into the competition. The first of a life time for the twin island. Following the matches against England, and Paraguay, they were eliminated from the tournament. Having internationally gained respect for having played their games courageously, boldly, and fearlessly.

Chapter Seventeen

I'd completed about six computer beginner courses at Preston College, but didn't fully grasp the concept. It wasn't until I saw an advert in our local newspaper regarding courses being held at Age Concern for two mornings a week. It was only then, that everything finally fell into place. Even so, I can only just cope with the basics.

"Good morning, Mrs Brathwaite." Dr Andrews said as we shook hands. She was a consultant neurologist. I almost had to fully extend my head with some discomfort to myself, to enable me to look into her hazelnut eyes, as we greeted each other. She wore a knee length grey skirt, with matching jacket and white blouse. With a smile that was in stark contrast to her outfit. As I took to my seat, she was turning around in her swivel chair, about to give me her un-divided attention. I fully explained to her how my accident occurred, and my problems since then. She arose to examine me. Finding that there was evidence of irritation or compression of the brachial plexus (a network of nerves which supply the chest, shoulder, and arms) which was more pronounced on the left side, than on the right. There was a lot of pain on touch, and pressure on the Brachial Plexus within the armpits. There was increased sensitivity within the 6th and 7th Cervical Vertebrae, supporting the head and neck and providing movement for them. Also, the 8th Cervical, and 1st Thoracic vertebrae which controls hand movements. Injury may cause partial or full loss of movement or feeling. She prescribed Lyrica 25 mgs daily. Lyrica is an anticonvulsant. Also used to treat pain caused by nerve damage. It was to be increased by a further 25 mgs every seven days, up to a dosage of 300 mgs daily. This was prescribed instead of Gabapentin, as I was unable to tolerate it previously, as it caused excessive drowsiness and dizziness. A cervical MRI scan was arranged by her, to rule

I Will Survive

out any abnormalities, along with a follow-up appointment after the scan to discuss its results.

A secluded restaurant and hotel, standing alone in a vast expanse of grass, flowers, and trees. Set apart from the country lane leading to Chipping. Ferrari's Country House Hotel and Restaurant, a family run business, was where The Sharoe Green Maternity Unit Reunion lunch was held annually. A time when all midwives from the unit, past and present, could gather, have lunch, and renew friendships. After our meal together, posing for photographs in the pleasant surrounding gardens of the venue as a memento of the occasion. Even at one event witnessing a bride and groom from a wedding party, arrive by helicopter.

"Thank God! There's a bus coming at last!" rejoiced the woman ahead of me in the queue at the bus stop. "You wait ages for a bus, then three come at once!" I remarked. Immediately, everyone waiting turned around to look at me. Their faces mirroring their thoughts, as they wondered what on earth I was talking about! There was only one bus approaching. I'd been experiencing difficulties with my vision. A visual impairment in which I saw one object as two or three.

Natalie and I had just boarded the No. 88A bus, taking us to the Odeon cinema. We'd planned to meet her school friend, Vicki there. No sooner had we taken our seats. I was desperate to pass urine. "I've only been to the toilet before I left home," I thought. By the time the bus had arrived in Cottam, I became extremely uncomfortable. Turning and twisting in my seat, whilst attempting to cross my legs. "What's wrong Mum?" asked Natalie. "I need to go to the toilet." I answered. "You've only just been." She replied. "Well, I need to go again." I explained. As we drove through Cottam, into Lea, and then into Ashton. I couldn't stand it any longer. I couldn't sit. "I'm going to wet myself." I thought. At this point, I stood up. Holding on to the metal bar of the bus, with my legs very tightly intertwined around it, as though they were stuck together with glue.

Natalie was making herself busy, listening to her music player. Very intent on looking through the window. I hopelessly tried to block the subtle glances coming my way from the passengers, from my mind. My primary intention was to prevent an accident occurring. Thankfully, there was a post office and an estate agent's at the next stop. I immediately pressed the bell. The bus couldn't come to a standstill soon enough. I alighted faster than

Usain Bolt! The" Bolt run" became the "John Wayne" walk, as I opened the estate agency door, entering the building. "May I …." Before I could complete the sentence, all three members of staff, without even saying a word, pointed in the direction of the staff toilet.

"Hmm!" Dr Hennessy mused as I sat in the dentist's chair having my check-up. "How long have your gums been bleeding profusely and are so puffy?" "Since I began taking Amlodipine a few weeks ago. "I answered. Amlodipine is a drug used to treat high blood pressure, by helping blood vessels to relax, so that the blood can flow through more easily. "Don't take any more of them. Contact your doctor as soon as possible." I'd received a message from my doctor's surgery requesting me to make an urgent appointment. I'd recently had blood tests done, prior to my diabetic review. My haemoglobin and Vitamin B12 levels had fallen dramatically. "I've been passing urine non-stop. I'm having double or triple vision. My gums have become swollen and are bleeding since taking Amlodipine. I had a dental check-up yesterday, and my dentist advised me to stop taking it." I informed Dr Boland. He was also overly concerned about my raised liver function tests. Immediately prescribing me a course of iron injections.

My arms were tied together with rope. They were dangling from rings of steel, hanging from a ceiling. I began to feel dizzy from the swaying of my body. A hot poker was being pierced into the left side of my neck. Then twisted and turned repeatedly, so that my neck muscles enveloped it. My arms began to feel as though they were no longer able to function, and that they would fall away from my body. Electrical currents were beginning to flow from the left side of my neck, downwards into my left shoulder, down my left arm, and hand. Where a nail was hammered into the middle of my palm. The electricity then flickers and flashes its way, in "Star Wars" fashion out through my fingers. At the same time, making their way upwards from the left side of my neck, around my left occiput, and into the left side of my face. I felt my left cheek being gently tickled, intermingled with being clobbered with a fist. As quickly as I'd fallen asleep, I'd awoken. Just managing to keep hold of my half-finished cup of tea. Totally confused. Unsure whether I'd been dreaming. My left arm, shoulder, neck, and face were aching.

Natalie and I had recently returned home from shopping at Asda. Some of the groceries required arm stretching to bring them from the taxi and to put them away. Feeling exhausted, I decided to have a cup of tea. Flopping onto my armchair, in front of the fire, to enjoy it in comfort. My arms were aching, as my nerve impulses were awakened by all this activity. I immediately telephoned Martha to make an appointment, which wasn't for another two hours. I chose to walk there, to calm myself. Walking through a nearby park, with hovering woodland, and a pond, with swans graciously floating on the still water, in the sunshine. The park was devoid of people. The children at school, and the adults at work.

Sitting on the swings for a while. Listening to my music, gently swaying along to the beats. One of my favourite calypsos began to play. Spontaneously arising from my seat, beginning to sing and dance. It was my own little concert. I was the entertainer, and the entertained. I sang at the top of my voice. Attempting to drown the effects of my pain.

Maureen was unable to avoid hearing me sing, as I approached Ambulant Physiotherapy. She was already prepared to deal with my entry. Roger, one of the physiotherapists employed there, was to perform the procedure, unable to remove the needles, as he was booked with another client. Therefore, following my twenty-minute sleep, Martha detached them after she'd dealt with another patron.

I'd received a letter from my solicitor that the court had recently held a direction hearing, so that they could ascertain how my claim would continue. My law firm had previously suggested that they make an application to the court to obtain further medical evidence. They'd instructed a barrister to attend on our behalf. To find out whether our application for additional medical evidence would be successful. It was agreed by them, that there was a possibility that I may have sustained a head injury, which could be responsible for my ongoing symptoms. They'd considered consulting a professor in neurology. It was stressed that should the professional's report be unsupportive of my claim. Then the offer of five thousand pounds in full and final settlement for pain, suffering, and loss of amenity be considered reasonable. Based upon the reports of the neurologist and the psychiatrist, I would be awarded nine thousand, five hundred pounds for financial losses. More if the professor's report was favourable.

It was drawn to my attention, that should my case be awarded a court hearing, and the judge be unaware of the offer to settle, then I could receive less than my offer. I wasn't hopeful that a professor of neurology would support me. Bearing all the information which I'd received in mind. I accepted the offer from the insurers of fourteen thousand, five hundred pounds of which four thousand pounds had to be repaid to my employers, in lieu of wages paid whilst off sick, as per terms and conditions of employment.

Chapter Eighteen

Since all my treatment options for high blood pressure had been undermined. I again enlisted the help of Catherine, the homeopath. Following another lengthy consultation. I was prescribed Crataegus. Commonly known as Hawthorn. Useful for cardiovascular disease and high blood pressure. Improving blood circulation to the heart and brain, decreasing blood lipids, the fat–like substance found in our blood and body tissues.

My prescribed treatment was the liquid Crataegus. Of which I was to follow the instructions very closely. Placing five drops of the tincture into a little water or fruit juice to drink once a day for two weeks, with intake of food or liquids prohibited to twenty minutes before and after drinking it. I followed the instructions religiously. Four weeks later, I began to feel dizzy and light-headed. I checked my blood pressure and the recordings had dropped considerably. I phoned Catherine, who advised me to stop taking the mixture.

My second application for ill health retirement was again declined. My physiotherapist also informed me about my neck scan results. There were multi-level cervical discs and facet joint degenerative changes and mild foraminal narrowing, with no significant neural compression.

The pounds were dropping off me! I was beginning to become concerned but pleased that I'd lost so much weight. I'd struggled with my heaviness since being diagnosed with an underactive thyroid. When breathlessness and tiredness began to accompany this. I made an appointment with my doctor. It took a long time for me to walk from the bus stop to the surgery. I was beginning to think that I'd never get there. I was puffing and blowing, as I dragged my swollen feet, with puffy ankles, along the pavement slabs.

Dressed in winter attire, three-layer thermal jacket, thermal underwear, hoodie, fleecy hat, a snood, and about five scarves, coiled around my neck. My glasses all steamed up as a result. It became increasingly difficult for me to breathe with every step that I took. Occasionally I was forced to stop walking and have a rest. Just to be able to get the air in and out of my lungs. Finally, it was mission accomplished! There was I standing at the door to the surgery. I attempted to open it, but it wouldn't budge. My body didn't have not one ounce of energy left in it. I continued to puff and blow uncontrollably. Someone rushed to my rescue, opening the door for me.

It was baby clinic afternoon. There were toddlers playing, and babies screaming after having their vaccinations. I could feel everyone's eyes fixated on me, as I removed my outer garments. One by one, putting them in my hat and scarf bag. "Would you like some water?" asked Dr Jones, as I'd developed a coughing fit which wouldn't go away. "I'm all right thanks." I replied, as I began drinking from my water bottle, which I now always carried with me. "I'm exhausted all the time. I feel so dreadful. I've never felt like this in my entire life. I've had a cold and cough that won't go away. There's a bubbly sensation in my lungs, and it feels as though my left lung is being pushed aside." I explained to him. Following a thorough medical examination, blood for full blood count, urea, electrolytes, liver function tests, referrals for a cardiogram and chest X ray were made.

Occasionally I would treat myself to an aromatherapy massage with the aid of oils. This totally relaxed my body, relieving my aches and pains. Restoring a sense of well-being to my body and mind. Improving my oxygen supply, increasing my blood circulation, and stimulating my immune system. I'd fall asleep as soon as my treatment commenced. The therapist would always advise me to top up my intake of water, as it aided the extraction of toxins from my body.

Taking the No 19 bus to the hospital, only five minutes walk from my home was my only option. I'd become so breathless, exhausted, and found it so difficult to walk anywhere. My chest Xray was scheduled for that day. I had to make a conscious effort to move my feet, as they felt like lead. Even though I was dressed in winter attire, I couldn't help but shiver. I felt as though I was stark naked. I'd become incapable of speaking as I eventually arrived at the reception desk at the X ray department. Only handing over to the secretarial assistant my appointment details. Flopping into the nearest

I Will Survive

seat available. Coughing uncontrollably. Grabbing my water bottle from my handbag, then attempting to place a medicated lozenge into my mouth. My chest X ray showed that there was evidence of upper lobe diversion. The upper pulmonary veins bigger than the lower ones, due to accumulation of blood, and bilateral hilar shadowing. Hilar being the vessels, bronchi, and lymph nodes, which expanded. Suggesting pulmonary oedema. The collection of fluid in the air spaces, and parts of the lung where gas transfer takes place.

With the first Xray being abnormal. I was required to have it repeated. Indicating an enlarged heart, with the interstitial changes in both lungs. Involving the lung tissue. Sustaining the air sacs of the lungs, with signs of early lamellar effusions at both lung bases. There was an abnormal collection of fluid between the surfaces of the lungs. Pulmonary sarcoidosis, where there is an abundance of unusually swollen cells was queried. My echogram performed due to the findings of an enlarged heart proved to be normal.

It was the 17$^{th\ of}$ May 2008.Cup final day and the day/ night walk the walk moon walk, held in London. There were walkers strolling in brightly coloured bras and clothing to raise money for breast cancer care and research. Hyde Park being the starting and finishing points of the event. Our midwives, Pauline, Carolynn, Roseann, Jan, and Sue eagerly set off. Leaving the carnival atmosphere, with the huge pink tent, with food, drink and music behind. The streets were overflowing with football fans, and revellers tumbling out of pubs and clubs. Welcoming in the serenity as dawn broke, against the historical, impressive, landmarks of the city. As they walked, messages of support trickled through via text messages and calls from the midwives at work. At the end of the trek, Carolynn slid down the trunk of a tree. Flopping on the grass. In tiredness, but happy that they`d achieved what they`d set out to do.

Two months had passed since my third application for NHS ill health retirement. On the basis that I was diagnosed with complex regional pain syndrome, and that after six years, a full recovery seemed very unlikely. On the 10^{tofh} February 2009, I presented myself at the chest clinic, being seen by Dr Hillman, consultant chest physician. He listened intently as I informed him of my symptoms. Worsening breathlessness, lingering cold and cough, feeling very unwell, and exhaustion. A referral for a CT thoracic scan, auto immune screen, 6minute walk test, and several blood tests were made. Pulmonary sarcoidosis was queried. My spirometry tests used to diagnose and check for any improvements and reactions to lung treatments, showed a reduced, obstructive, restrictive defect. M y weight and height were measured before the tests were done. I was required to breathe into the spirometer. First taking a deep breath in, then placing my lips tightly around the mouthpiece. A clip was attached to my nose, ensuring that no air escaped. The tests examine how the lungs work, and how effective breathing in and out is. The tests proved very difficult for me to perform. The clip continually slipping from my nose, as the coughing persisted. Finding it difficult to breathe.

Instead of telephoning the finance department concerning the progress of my successful NHS ill health retirement claim. I visited it instead. My application was completed. It had been transferred to the NHS pensions agency at Fleetwood. For them to administer the finishing touches. I wasn't looking forward to my six-minute walk test, determining how I can easily walk at my normal pace, within a six-minute period. Mine was a disaster. Regularly interrupting the assessment to sit to have a rest. My oxygen evaluation was surprisingly within normal limits, Therefore, I didn't require any oxygen.

Soon after I attended the scan department for an imaging Xray portraying pictures of my chest and upper abdomen. I was required to lie on a slender table, which slid into the centre of a cave- like scanner. I closed my eyes. Trying to relax as much as I could. Taking deep breaths then breathing out slowly, At the same time lying still so that the procedure could be completed as quickly as possible. I was instructed by the radiographer to hold my breath to effectively take the pictures. The full process took only a few minutes. There was an enlargement of the hila, the vessels, bronchi, lymph nodes, and the trachea. Pulmonary sarcoidosis was suspected. In view of this, I was referred for a bronchoscopy and biopsy to confirm diagnosis and treatment.

I couldn't stop coughing and attempting to clear my throat. Feeling more and more uncomfortable and agitated. I found it difficult to keep still. I was very relaxed and drowsy from the effects of Midazolam 3 milligrams intra venously. An anaesthetic used as a sedative to induce rest. However, in my stupor, I began to experience this overwhelming desire to resist this irritable intrusion of someone attempting to push this piece of tubing down my nostril, and into my airways. I was lying on the treatment bed in the bronchoscopy department, as a day case patient. About to have a bronchoscopy, via a bronchoscope. A flexible fibre optic tubing, with a camera at the end, which visualises the tissues of the lungs, with specimens taken from the posterior segment of the right upper lobe. Using additional anaesthetic, Lignocaine gel to make the process less painful. Despite this, the coughing, clearing of my throat and restlessness continued. Making it more difficult for the clinicians to carry out. The tests proved to be abnormal. Supporting the diagnosis of pulmonary sarcoidosis.

"I've got it! I've got it!" I declared, as there on the ATM machine was the proof! My bank balance had dramatically improved! My ill health NHS retirement pension had been completely settled. And about time too.

Chapter Nineteen

My body continued to itch. I was applying Calamine Lotion to soothe it, as my feelings of drowsiness persisted. I'd recently been prescribed Methotrexate. Used for the treatment of sarcoidosis, preventing rapid regrowth of the body's cells.

"Mum, stop taking these tablets immediately!" stated Edward and Natalie. "Whilst you were out Dr Hillman called to say that your liver function test results were very high. You must discontinue Methotrexate at once." To reinforce that statement. A letter promptly arrived in the post the following morning from him, informing me that my liver function tests were deranged. I was to discontinue taking the tablet immediately. In its place Azathioprine was ordered, with similar effects. This too was quickly stopped. I was becoming increasingly concerned about my condition. I knew that should I continue taking any more of these tablets, that they could eventually shorten my life.

My curiosity was getting the better of me. For the past few months, I'd noticed a business unit operating within the Guild Hall Shopping Arcade. Above its entrance was a bright blue sign, running over the length of its doorway, conveying the word "Ceragem." Also, in bold blue lettering. I'd also observed many people coming and going through its doors. Too busy gazing at the entrance, I'd almost collided with a friend of mine. "Hi Jennifer." I uttered. Before she could respond, I'd asked her. "What's all this about?" "It's a Ceragem Centre which opened four months ago. It's a massage treatment bed. Good for all sorts of ailments and pain. The sessions are free, and last forty minutes." As she explained this to me, she offered me a leaflet to read, defining the benefits of the equipment.

The first of its kind in the U, K. Based in Preston. Following in the footsteps of having the first motorway, The M6 and K.F.C. Originating in South Korea. Using a combination of modern technology, and traditional Eastern medicinal theories. Improving general health and wellbeing. Using heat to aid healing and relaxation. Increasing blood flow, Stimulating pressure points in the body. Acupressure like acupuncture is applied to special points along the spine. As the jade stones moved up and down my spine, it felt very uncomfortable. When the region around my occiput and shoulders were being massaged, the pain relief was unremarkably like that of my monthly acupuncture sessions. I felt very relaxed. As though I was floating and care-free. As the session came to an end. I knew that this was what I was praying and longing for. Acupuncture every day! As I arose from the bed, I announced to Julie, who organized the sessions along with Geoff. "God must have sent you!"

I began visiting the centre six days a week. Monday through Saturday. With my reliance on my pain killers diminishing, helping me to manage my pain more effectively. I realised also that by placing the jade stones on my chest. I could slowly but surely feel the fluid disappearing from my lungs, improving my breathlessness and coughing.

My brother Charles, wife, Sabrina, and daughter Alex, who lived in Trinidad. Were on holiday in mainland Europe, including England. He travelled from London to visit our family here in Preston. It was with great joy that I told him to expect Eddie and me in March 2010. I'd noticed an advert in the daily newspaper, regarding a two-week Caribbean cruise and immediately booked it.

"None of the usual treatments are suitable for me, and I'm unwilling to attempt any others, due to the unwanted side effects. I've recently started using a massage bed which applies acupressure to points along my spine, helping with pain relief. The usage of jade stones also aids healing, of which I'm already slowly feeling the effects. I would like to persevere with this." I revealed to Dr Hillman at my follow-up appointment. "I realise what your concerns are, and I'm happy for you to continue with what you've been using." He reassured me. Just two weeks following Lillian's 82nd birthday. Pat informed me that she'd passed away. Returning to London for her funeral after seeing her only two weeks before.

"Your spirometry, measurements of the breathing capacity of the lungs, shows improvement, but there remains some mild obstruction within the lungs. Your oxygen saturation levels are 95% in room air. I wish you well for your holiday." Dr Hillman remarked at my review appointment shortly before I travelled. Junnet, our four-year-old neighbour, who lived across the road from us, burst into tears as I bid her and her family farewell. Since she was a baby, she'd become very close to our family, so I'd called her my adopted grand-daughter. Full of excitement I was unable to sleep that night. Having to awaken in the early hours of the morning for our taxi to Preston train station, then onwards to Manchester Airport. Wednesday the 10th of March had arrived. I'd had an acupuncture session with Martha the evening before, to help me cope with the long trans-Atlantic flight. I was overjoyed to be visiting the Caribbean once again. To renew acquaintances with family and friends, and to enjoy the sun, sea, sand and cuisine. Boarding a Thomas Cook chartered flight to Bridgetown, Barbados, where several other aircrafts coming from Gatwick and Heathrow Airports had already landed. Their passengers ready to board the buses waiting on the tarmac, to take us to the Bridgetown docks from the airport in Christchurch. From whence we were to embark the cruise liner, "Ocean Village." As I'd descended the metal stairway to our bus, my body transformed from being in pain, stiffness and imprisonment, to that of a bird set free, as my body absorbed the abundant sunlight and warm weather.

A professional photograph of Eddie and me was taken by the ship's photographer, on the gangplank, as we embarked. Arriving some thirty minutes later to our cabin. Our home for the next two weeks, with colourful, vivid views of the outside world, captured from our porthole. Halfway through our leisurely unpacking, came the shrilly sound of the emergency muster drill. In order to prepare passengers for safe evacuation, whilst on board the ship. We gathered our life jackets, proceeding in an orderly fashion to the muster station. Where we were met by the captain, other crew members, and hundreds of other passengers. Where the emergency exit procedure was demonstrated, and we were each required to practise donning our life jackets the correct way.

Elegantly and comfortably dressed in shiny black / silver top and black trousers, complimented with black sandals. Eddie wearing a blue and white striped shirt, blue tie, black trousers, and black shoes. Emerging from our cabin, strolling towards the stairway, mid vessel, to the James Martin Bistro, on the floor above. Where we were booked to dine at 8.30. P.M. The bright lights of the Barbadian nightlife twinkled from ashore. We weren't due to leave the island until midnight, due to refuelling, and stocking up with water for the first week's journey. Feeling very relaxed, and stress free, we were ready and waiting to enjoy everything that was coming our way. Following our meal, the sound of karaoke music and singing led us to a bar, next to the Oval Pub, where there was a gathering of people experiencing a party atmosphere. With all of us shouting "hooray "at the stroke of midnight, as the "Ocean Village" left the shores of Barbados.

At breakfast that morning, we were sat within view of the huge windows of the Waterfront Restaurant, awed by the vast ocean on which our ship was afloat. Our first day was being spent at sea. I was eager to venture down to Charlie's internet café to correspond with Richard and Claudette, our friends who we were due to meet on the 17 of March in Barbados. And family and friends gathering in Tobago from Trinidad on the 19th of March. Already booked in for a head, neck, and shoulder aromatherapy massage, I found my way to the treatment room with great difficulty, having to ask someone to guide me there. Meeting Eddie, Roy and Barbara, who we'd met on the previous evening, for a few drinks in the Oval Pub.

Friday the 12th of March dawned bright and beautiful. From our cabin we observed colourful buildings, with lush, green hillsides positioned beyond them. We couldn't wait to get dressed, have breakfast, and get ashore. Before long we were seated in a maxi taxi alongside some other passengers. Experiencing life on Tortola. There were hills everywhere. Eventually arriving at Cane Garden Bay. There were swaying palm trees, fine white sand, turquoise/blue water, surrounded by flourishing green tropical planted hillsides. There was an array of restaurants, shops, bars, and water sports companies plying their trades.

Back in the centre of Road Town, Tortola's capital was the J.R O'Neal Botanical Gardens, one of the best of the Caribbean. There was an array of luxuriant green, lavish plants, and exotic trees and herbs. Particularly of interest to me was a bright, red Hibiscus plant. Having pride of place, standing like royalty in the middle of a host of other plants. Amongst the four acres of land, there was a lily pond, tropical bird houses, and a gazebo of orchids. There was also a nursery storing endangered species.

Ensuring their survival. On the way back to the liner Natalie rang. Junnet had demanded to speak to me. She didn't believe that we were away on holiday.

Awoken abruptly by the bright rays of sunshine threatening to escape from the outside world, beyond our cabin, through the drawn curtains of our suite. Prompting me to pull them apart. Revealing a bright blue sky, with not a cloud in sight. As on Tortola, there were colourful buildings around the quayside. We'd docked in Phillipsburg. The capital of St Maarten early that morning. Immediately on disembarking, the sound of the alluring music from a small group of men, playing their steel drums. Drifting down the quayside, as we walked along to the beat of the drums. Next to where our liner docked, was a beautiful, white sandy beach. Surrounded by palm trees, with serene blue/ green waters, lapping against the shore. The "Ocean Village," as well as other ships, were clearly visible in the distance. After spending about one blissful hour in the water, I sat on the sand, with the waves gently overlapping my feet, watching the world go by. Wishing that that special moment would never end. Eddie showed no interest in joining me, but was sat on a nearby bench, also enjoying the occasion. After an hour, we were no longer the sole occupants of the beach. It was now alive with people from the seaside's hotels, bars and restaurants, lining the entire length of this delightful plage. Venturing into the French side of the island, by a $4.00return taxi ride. Returning to Philipsburg a few hours later. Getting back to the liner with adequate time for the 5P.M departure from the island.

Very quickly, the maxi taxi we were already seated in, filled with passengers from the various cruise ships at the quayside, at Basseterre, St kitts. It was the morning of the 14th of March2010. Being a Sunday, Independence Square, one of the capital's main streets, where both Catholic and Anglican churches were situated, was very busy with people attending services. A visit to the internationally acclaimed Caribelle Batik and its gardens was not to be missed. Producing wonderful batik products, with gift items being available for sale at the gift shop. The island, volcanic in nature was made evident by its peaks, built up by its own eruptions. Taking pride of place in the city is Warner Park Cricket Ground. Famous for hosting four matches of the 2007 cricket world cup. Our taxi driver dropping us off at the beach, after visiting Fairview Guest House and gardens. Once home to the great grandfather of Virginia Woolf. Giving us ample time for swimming and having lunch. Before taking us back to the docks, for the boarding of our respective ships.

Our first week was almost at an end. It was already Monday the 15th of March, and we were presently anchored in St John's Antigua. Making our way through an archway of bustling boutiques, bars, café`s, restaurants, and souvenir shops. Finding a taxi proved easy once again. Giving us a tour of the island. Driving past the Antigua Recreation Ground, where Brian Lara scored his records of 375, and 400 runs against England. About a twenty-minute drive away was the Sir Vivian Richards Stadium in North Sound.

As with most of the Caribbean Islands, there was an abundance of rain forests, with plenty of fruits, vegetables, and plants. Now in South Antigua, and to our right, was the horse-shoe shaped Falmouth Harbour, where several yachts were moored. Nearby was Nelson's Dockyard. Named after Admiral Horatio Nelson, where some of Antigua's sailing and yachting events are held. Finally dropping us off, after arranging to meet us later, for return to the ship, at one of the most beautiful beaches I'd ever seen. An alluring resort, with a bar and café/ restaurant. The aroma of freshly cooked food, surrounded by white sand, clean calm blue/ aquamarine waters, with the leaves of the coconut trees waving gently in the slightly breezy sunshine.

On the following morning, we anchored a few miles offshore, requiring all passengers disembarking to board a boat, taking them to Roseau, the capital of Dominica. Unsettled over the past few days by an allergic reaction. Causing a gradual increase in the size of my lips. Resulting in them becoming huge, red, sore, and very itchy. My immediate intent on landing, was to find the nearest pharmacy. This we did as soon as our feet touched the earth. I'd been taking Piriton, with no effect. The pharmacist recommended another antihistamine. Advising me to request medical aid, as soon as possible should my condition worsen. Taking the required dosage at once. We then boarded a taxi amongst other passengers from the various liners visiting the island. As we drove along, I could feel myself becoming sleepy, but I continued to try to keep myself awake, to enjoy the Dominican experience. As my lips began to feel less swollen.

There were many waterfalls, rivers, and hot springs on the mountainous, lush, rain forest type vegetation. With adventure trails for the very enterprising visitors. About twenty miles from Roseau, were the famous twin Trafalgar Waterfalls. To the left was "The Father," and to the right, "The Mother." The more adventurous amongst us were encouraged to continue walking. To swim in the waters of "The Mother" where there was a hot spring.

Aware that we were keen followers of cricket. The driver was very eager to point out Windsor Park. Serving the dual purpose of a national stadium, and cricket. I was becoming more and more sleepy. Desperate to return to the confines of the ship. Recovering in time for dinner, and the last evening between us, Roy and Barbara, who'd commenced their holiday the week before us. Bidding each other farewell at the end of the evening. Exchanging telephone numbers and addresses. Promising to keep in touch.

There was Richard standing at the entrance to the docks. Exactly where we'd arranged to meet. We hadn't seen each other in twenty-eight years. Not since he, his wife, Claudette, and their two beautiful children, Richard, four years, and daughter, Karen, eighteen months, had relocated to Barbados, where Richard was born, from London. There was someone standing next to him. Eddie and I found it impossible to believe that that person was Richard Jr. We hadn't seen him since he was four! Richard Jr. who worked at the docks, was on his way to work. We bid him hello and farewell almost at the same time. Promising that we'd meet up with him and his wife Gail later that day. Spending almost an hour at Richard's home in St Philip, then visiting Karen, a doctor, at her own private practise. Having not seen her since she was eighteen months old. Fortunately, there weren't any patients at the time to interrupt our little reunion. Claudette, her mother, and part time receptionist joined us for lunch, and the activities for the rest of the day.

We were about to begin a tour of this beautiful island. Passing through the centre of the city, Broad Street. The shopping hub of Bridgetown. Evident by the volume of shoppers in the area. Once again, we saw the statue of Sir Garfield Sobers, and the Kensington Oval cricket ground. Stopping off for lunch, before continuing our drive along Barbados's rugged coastline. Bathsheba, with its delightful, white, sandy beaches, and formations of rock, from which the waves of the Atlantic Ocean beat upon. Breaking up, and forming layers of white foam, rich in minerals. Through Bath, another lovely beach on the East coast, then St Andrews, St George, Christ Church, then St Philip, viewing the white Georgian mansion, Sam Lord Castle.

Stopping off at a restaurant for an evening meal. Reunited again with Karen, and another friend Will, who lived and worked in London, but now residing in Canada. He'd arrived in the country on holiday on the previous day. My anti histamines had done a marvellous job. My lips had decreased in size tremendously. Remaining slightly itchy. It also left me feeling very tired by the end of the day, which was unfortunate, as the ship wasn't leaving the port until midnight. I couldn't keep my eyes opened any longer. Therefore, Richard took us back to Bridgetown about 7.30P.M. We promised that we would see them again on our return there, on the following Wednesday. For our return to Manchester, England.

Chapter Twenty

Having left Barbados at midnight, and a day at sea. We arrived in Scarborough, Tobago on Friday the 19th of March. There to meet us at the docks were two of my sisters, Pam and Pat, brother Charles, wife Sabrina, another brother, Skippy, wife Joanne, son, Joshua, fourteen, and childhood friend, Arlene.

Pam, Pat, and Arlene took me clothes shopping at a nearby shopping mall. Picking up some pre-cooked food from the home of Pat's friend, who was a caterer. We then all gathered at their apartment at Jimmy's. Blocks of holiday flats, a few minutes' walk from Store Bay, and Pigeon Point, where they were staying for the weekend. Kitts, a friend of ours who'd lived and worked in London, and returned to live in Trinidad, met us there, after arriving in Tobago that morning by aeroplane.

We all enjoyed our lunch of Cou-Cou, (consisting of corn meal and okra) callaloo, (mixture of spinach, or dasheen leaves, okra, coconut milk) chicken, crab, plantains, yam, and other vegetables, and salad. By then, we were all eager to visit Store Bay, in close proximity to the airport. A popular, delightful, white sandy beach, with clear blue waters. Deck chairs and umbrellas spread along the sand. An abundance of food outlets, bars, and restaurants surrounding it.

Already in the water were my cousins, Margaret, and her sister, Pat, who live in Canada. They were holidaying in Trinidad and Tobago. There was a hive of activity, with vacationers boarding glass bottomed boats, taking them to Buccoo Reef and Nylon Pool. Another shallow body of still water, lying just beyond the reef. A short distance away from Store Bay, and Pigeon Point.

It was soon time to return to Jimmy's for a shower, change of clothing, and family pictures taken by Arlene, who was a photographer. We also made a birthday telephone call to our sister, Judy, who lived in Maryland, U.S. A. Regrettably, it was time to return to Scarborough. Leaving my family and friends behind, as we boarded "The Ocean Village" for the five P.M departure was sad and heart breaking. We disappeared to the top deck to have a better view of our departure from Tobago's shores. My loved ones went to Arlene's home, where she lives on a hill, for a bird's eye view, where they stood until the vessel passed out of their sight over the horizon.

As we disembarked on the following morning, we noticed that there wasn't a jetty or any taxis around. We'd docked at El-Guamache Port, Isla Margarita. We hadn't booked any trips for any of the islands. Depending on our own form of transport. Unable to view any, we followed the other passengers, who all turned right on leaving the ship. Heading to a small, shallow beach. Accessible from the port via stalls selling jewellery, art, t-shirts, and souvenirs, bars and a restaurant, with picnic tables and dried palm shaped leaves, spread like umbrellas over them, along the pathway.

During the early hours of Sunday the 21st of March, we'd arrived at St Lucia. Soon after breakfast, we comfortably sat in our taxi to begin our tour of the island. Near the town of Soufriere, in volcanic grandeur, stood the twin peaks, The Pitons. Gros and Petit. A world heritage site. Mountainous and steeple like. Regally rising from the sea. Nearby was Fond Doux Estate, where acres of cocoa, bananas, coconuts, and citrus fruit trees are cultivated.

Driving through the island's rain forest, walking and biking tours were in evidence. For the most adventurous, were Krypton Factor style zip wire rides, across the dense, ever green forests. To the North of the island is Gros Islet, much flatter, and less volcanic than the south. Nearby, was The Beausejour cricket stadium, where many local and international matches take place.

On the following morning, we arrived in St Georges Grenada. A powerhouse of movement as we went ashore. The café's bars, and souvenir shops were jam packed, as we joined the queue with our many purchases. Visiting the market square, opposite the cruise terminal, where we bought a small memento of Grenada. A straw basket of cloves, nutmeg, cinnamon, and orange peel. As the island is also known as the island of spice. The harbour was strikingly beautiful. Somewhat horseshoe shaped, with many colourful houses surrounding it. At the northern end, were bright multi coloured boats, and grey/ black Georgian houses. Wanting to visit Grand Anse Beach, we flogged down a passing taxi to take us there.

Grand Anse Beach, considered to be one of the best in the world, and a popular tourist attraction. Encircled by hotels, with its fine white sand, and blue sea. Bars, café`s, and coconut and almond trees providing refuge from the mid-day sun. It was a sense of pure joy to frolic in the water. Sitting at the water`s edge, whilst the waves gently rolled over my feet. The most pleasurable part of the afternoon was when someone entertaining the tourists by strumming his guitar, and singing calypsos, stood next to me, singing one of my favourite childhood ditties. "The Lizard." I very quickly sprang to my feet, joining him in singing and dancing.

It was the last day of our cruise and the 23rd of March. Arriving early that morning in Kingstown, the capital of St Vincent. On the following morning, on landing in Barbados. We were due to leave the ship for the airport, and our return journey to Manchester. Our suitcases had to be packed and ready that evening. To be left outside our cabin, to be collected for transfer to the airport. With this in mind, we decided not to wander far from the docks. Instead strolling around nearby streets. Enjoying some drinks with locals in a bar, discussing West Indies cricket past and present.

Later that evening, as we were dining at the exclusive top deck restaurant. The liner appeared to be heading towards Bridgetown at an enormous speed. The water in the swimming pool was swishing about from side to side. Evidently someone had died on board, and we needed to get there very quickly. Immediately after breakfast, we were required to present our passports for Immigration control. Followed hours later by departure from the vessel by flight number and departure time from the airport. As we got off the coach, Richard, Claudette, and Will were there waiting for us outside the terminal building. We enjoyed a chat and a few drinks before bidding each other farewell, for our departure to Manchester.

Landing at Manchester Airport at 6.30 on the following early spring morning, was quite a change from the warmth of the Caribbean. Arriving in Preston by train, several hours later. Edward, Natalie and Junnet were happy to see us. Eager to receive what gifts we`d bought for them. We were happy to be back in Preston, but sorry to have left our respective homelands behind. Continuing to attend the Ceragem Centre six days a week. Relieved and reassured that its usage had improved my quality of life in so many ways,

I Will Survive

by helping to ease my pain. Similar in action to that of acupuncture. Using jade stones to massage special points along the spine. Releasing blocked energy, promoting its flow. Helping to restore body balance, using heat to aid healing. Relieving the effects of aches and pain. Helping me not to be dependent on my analgesia.

My general health and well-being had definitely been improved. I felt more awake, and not in a Zombie–like state twenty–four hours a day. Eventually deciding to purchase a bed. Having it delivered and set up by Geoff, just before Easter 2010. My dream had come true! I could have acupuncture every day now. And what a difference it made! I looked and felt more alert than I'd done in a long time. I felt more confident as I was able to manage my condition better. My lung function was improving. There was no extreme breathlessness, or dreadful cough. My spirometry and lung volume within normal limits but at a reduced transfer rate. This determines the ability of the lungs to transport blood throughout the body of 67%. Higher than the previous year. Pleased with my progress, Dr Hillman wished to see me again in eight months time. In which my discharge from the chest clinic was a possibility. Eight months later at my clinic review, my chest Xray was an improvement to the previous one. Not perfect, but the best that it would ever be. Dr Hillman reassured me. The spirometry lung volume was improving. He was happy to discharge me from his care.

I've come to realise that having my accident at the time I did was a blessing in disguise. At that time, I felt very unwell. My body overworked, and stressful. Something more sinister could have occurred in its place. My injuries aren't as traumatic as when they'd first appeared, as I have ascertained how to cope with them. Life has taught me so much from my birth to the present day. It is in adversity that I learnt to survive by conquering my fears, and to triumph as a result. To be the victor instead of the victim.

About the Author

Helen Brathwaite qualified as a State Registered Nurse in 1978, a State Certified Midwife in 1980, and a Registered Mental Nurse in 1982. Helping to influence her lifestyle choices, as her sensitive body reacted negatively to certain medicinal drugs. Causing tiredness, drowsiness, and elevated liver function tests. Her grandmother has also impacted her thoughts towards the usage of alternative forms of treatments such as aromatherapy, and acupuncture, in association with other conforming medicines, as she was a great believer in homeopathy. She has no previous literary experiences, but has been inspired to impart to others her personal story, that they would be encouraged also.

www.ingramcontent.com/pod-product-compliance
Lightning Source LLC
LaVergne TN
LVHW091556060526
838200LV00036B/861